Benjamin Franklin Tillinghast

Three cities, and their industrial interests,

With an historical and descriptive sketch of the national armory and arsenal, the location, manufacturing facilities, and business advantages of Davenport, Iowa, Rock Island and Moline, Illinois

Benjamin Franklin Tillinghast

Three cities, and their industrial interests,
With an historical and descriptive sketch of the national armory and arsenal, the location, manufacturing facilities, and business advantages of Davenport, Iowa, Rock Island and Moline, Illinois

ISBN/EAN: 9783337713614

Printed in Europe, USA, Canada, Australia, Japan

Cover: Foto ©ninafisch / pixelio.de

More available books at **www.hansebooks.com**

The Davenport National Bank.

DEPOSITORY OF THE UNITED STATES.

DAVENPORT, IOWA.

CAPITAL, - - - $200,000.

OFFICERS.

E. S. BALLORD, President.　　　S. F. SMITH, Vice-President.
G. E. MAXWELL, Cashier.　　　C. A. MAST, Asst. Cashier.

DIRECTORS.

HON. H. PRICE.　　　WM. RENWICK.　　　W. D. PETERSEN.
J. B. PHELPS.　　　I. H. SEARS.　　　E. S. BALLORD.
　　　GEO. H. FRENCH.　　　S. F. SMITH.

CITIZENS NATIONAL BANK
—— OF ——

DAVENPORT, IOWA.

CAPITAL, - - - - $100,000.00
SURPLUS, - - - - $100,000.00

OFFICERS.

F. H. GRIGGS, President.　　　E. S. CARL, Cashier.
ROBERT KRAUSE, Vice-President.　　　ADOLPH PRIESTER, Asst. Cashier.

DIRECTORS.

T. W. McCLELLAND.　　　NICHOLAS KUHNEN.　　　F. H. GRIGGS.
ROBERT KRAUSE.　　　P. T. KOCH.　　　D. GOULD.
OTTO ALBRECHT.　　　D. N. RICHARDSON.　　　H. H. ANDRESEN.
　　　W. C. WADSWORTH.

A GENERAL BANKING BUSINESS TRANSACTED. FOREIGN EXCHANGE SOLD AT THE LOWEST RATES.

WE ISSUE OUR OWN DRAFTS ON ALL THE PRINCIPAL CITIES OF EUROPE.

GERMAN SAVINGS BANK,

DAVENPORT, IOWA.

CAPITAL, $230,000.   SURPLUS, $30,000.

Five Per Cent Interest Paid on Deposits.

MONEY LOANED ON REAL ESTATE & PERSONAL SECURITY.

Office open from 9 A. M. to 3 P. M., and on Saturdays to 8 P. M.

OFFICERS.

H. LISCHER, President.   L. WAHLE, Vice-President.
H. H. ANDRESEN, Cashier.
JAS. F. BREDOW, Asst. Cashier.   G. G. CARSTENS, Attorney.

DIRECTORS.

OTTO ALBRECHT.	N. KUHNEN.	J. M. LYTER.
H. H. ANDRESEN.	H. LISCHER.	H. TECHENTIN.
D. GOULD.	J. LORENZEN.	L. WAHLE.

THE DAVENPORT SAVINGS BANK,

DAVENPORT, IOWA.

PAID-UP CAPITAL,   -   -   - $120,000.00

OFFICERS.

C. E. PUTNAM, President.   R. SMETHAM, Secretary and Cashier.
LOUIS HALLER, Vice-President.   JOHN B. MEYER, Asst. Cashier.

DIRECTORS.

JAMES GRANT.	CHARLES E. PUTNAM.	AUGUST STEFFEN.
HENRY KOHRS.	W. O. SCHMIDT.	J. D. MORRISON.
LOUIS HALLER.	S. F. SMITH.	RICHARD SMETHAM.

W. C. WADSWORTH & CO.

109, 111 & 113 EAST SECOND STREET,

DAVENPORT, IOWA,

IMPORTERS AND JOBBERS OF

DRY GOODS

HOSIERY,

Notions, Underwear, Etc.

Our Stock is New and Inviting, and Complete in Every Department.

We Guarantee Prices as LOW as any quotations offered in Chicago or New York.

We carry the CHOICEST STOCK OF PRINTS and the BEST BRANDS OF DOMESTICS to be found in the West.

SPECIAL ATTENTION GIVEN TO ORDERS.

Hastings, White & Fisher

❈PHOTOGRAPHERS❈

OLD PICTURES COPIED AND ENLARGED — FINISHED IN CRAYON, INK, AND PASTEL.

MANUFACTURERS AND DEALERS IN

❈PICTURE-FRAMES❈

GOLD FRAMES A SPECIALTY.   ALL WORK WARRANTED FIRST-CLASS.

320 Brady Street,   Davenport, Iowa.

ESTABLISHED 1865.

COAL AND LIME

J. S. WYLIE,

SHIPPER OF HARD AND SOFT COAL, WHITE LIME, ETC.

RATES OBTAINED FOR DELIVERY IN CAR LOTS TO ALL POINTS IN THE NORTHWEST.

HARD COAL ALL RAIL FROM MINES.

217 BRADY ST.　　　　DAVENPORT, IOWA.

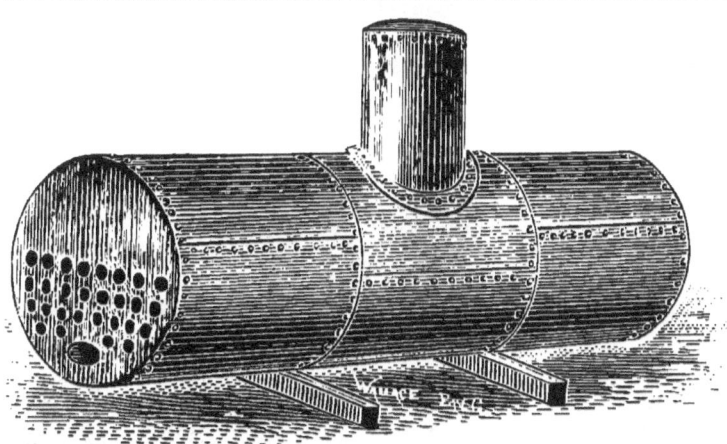

DAVENPORT BOILER WORKS
GRUPE & MURRAY, Proprietors.

All kinds of Boilers, Lard Tanks, Water Tanks, Smoke Stacks, Breechings, and Sheet Iron Work manufactured to order. Also Vault Doors, Iron Shutters, and Jail Work. Particular attention given to Repairing.

Orders by Mail or Telegraph promptly attended to.

Shop, 317 East Second Street, near Government Bridge,　　　DAVENPORT, IOWA.

LAND & LOAN OFFICE
—OF—
CHAS. H. KENT,
DAVENPORT, IOWA.

Special attention given to settling of Estates.

Davenport Property and Iowa Lands a Specialty.

Dwellings, Stores, and Farms for Sale or Rent.

Taxes Paid for Non-Residents in City or in any County in Iowa.

Safe Investments made in First Mortgages on Improved Real Estate, worth double the amount loaned.

All letters of inquiry as to the advantages of Davenport as a manufacturing point, railroad and river facilities, and all business entrusted to my care will meet with prompt attention.

SPECIAL TO MANUFACTURERS.

I have in my agency some choice mill sites, from one to twenty acres, with good shipping facilities by river or rail. To corporations or individuals who may wish to establish any manufacturing industry of merit, the most liberal terms will be given.

RESIDENCE PROPERTY.

I have some very desirable residences for sale low; also, building sites, which may be had at reasonable figures. Corporations requiring several blocks or ground for erecting dwellings for their operatives can be accommodated.

MARK THIS.

Real estate in Davenport will never be lower. Those who take advantage of present low prices cannot fail in making a profitable investment. Our predictions are based upon twenty-five years experience in the real estate business, and we believe we are competent to judge by the knowledge of the past. With the present outlook and demand, we are confident that real estate in Davenport is the best-paying investment now offered.

SAFE INVESTMENTS

Made on first-class Iowa real estate; first mortgages, worth three times amount loaned; interest payable semi-annually, at Boston or New York. Security and prompt payments guaranteed equal to any in New England or any of the Eastern States.

TWENTY-FIVE YEARS

We have been actively engaged in the real estate business, having now the care of many valuable estates, worth from $5,000 to $100,000, acting in the capacity either as agent, administrator, executor, guardian, or trustee, which gives us special advantages and opportunities of knowing the value of real estate, with the general character and standing of applicants for loans. Not a loan that we have placed has ever been lost, or in any way compromised.

RATE OF INTEREST.

A medium rate of interest is best for the lender and borrower. A high rate of interest does not command the best securities or prompt payments of interest and principal. We shall be pleased to correspond with corporations, administrators, guardians, insurance companies, or individuals, who may have surplus funds to invest.

CHAS. H. KENT, Land & Loan Agent, Davenport, Iowa.

LARGEST BOOK HOUSE ON THE UPPER MISSISSIPPI. ESTABLISHED 1858.

CRAMPTON & CO.
WHOLESALE AND RETAIL DEALERS IN
Books, Stationery, Wall Paper and Fancy Goods.
MANUFACTURERS OF FIRST-CLASS
——— BLANK BOOKS ———
For County Officers, Bankers, Merchants, and Manufacturers. PRICE AND QUALITY GUARANTEED.

ROCK ISLAND, ILLINOIS.

IMPROVED SAFETY
PASSENGER AND FREIGHT ELEVATORS

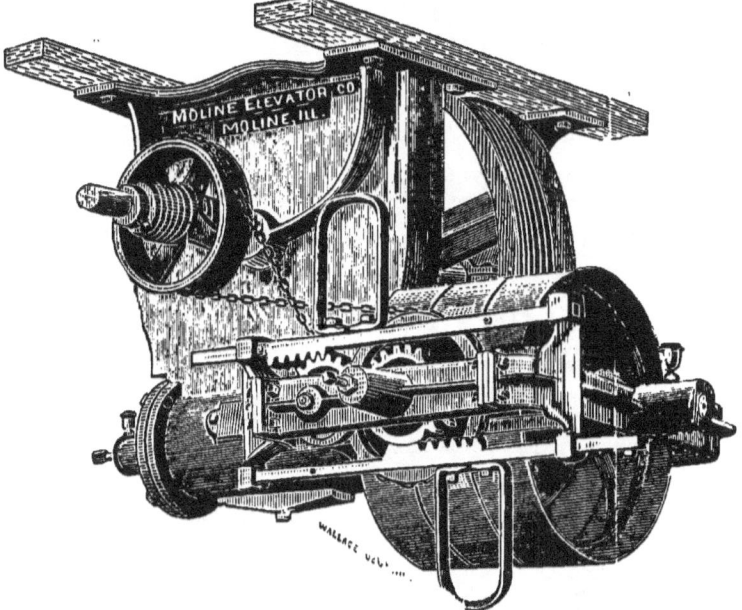

Center Lift, Hydraulic, Steam, Gas, and Hand Power.
AUTOMATIC HATCH DOOR. BEST ELEVATOR MADE.

Refer, by permission, to Sieg & Williams (who use gas engine), Geo. H. Young & Co., Eagle Steam Bakery, Eagle Manufacturing Co., Dessaint & Sons, Davenport; Barnard & Leas Manufacturing Co., Moline Plow Co., Deere & Co., Williams, White & Co., D. O. Reid, Dr. P. L. McKinnie, Moline; B. D. Buford & Co., Hawley & Hill, Rock Island; Milan Wagon Works, Milan, Ill.

Moline Elevator Co., Builders, Moline, Ill.

D. H. HARTWELL, Pres. J. C. EMEIS, V.-Pres. and Supt. A. F. CUTTER, Sec. and Treas.

Davenport Steam Heating Co.

Steam Warming and Ventilating Apparatus for Public and Private Buildings. STEAM ENGINES, PUMPS, and BOILERS. All kinds of Machine Work promptly done by best of mechanics. Agents for the Haxtun Patent Base Burning Boilers for low pressure work, for either soft or hard coal. Also agents for the celebrated Gibbs & Sterrett Manufacturing Company's Steam Engines, Crane Steam Pump, Torrent Boiler Feed Pumps, and Otto Silent Gas Engines. Outfits for Creameries furnished on short notice. Correspondence solicited.

Junction Third and Front Sts.   DAVENPORT, IOWA.

— ESTABLISHED AUGUST 15TH, 1864. —

ROBERT KRAUSE,
WHOLESALE AND RETAIL DEALER IN

Clothing, Cloths and Trimmings,

GENTLEMEN'S FURNISHING GOODS,
— AND —
Manufacturer of Pantaloons, Shirts, and Overalls,

125 AND 127 EAST SECOND STREET,   DAVENPORT, IOWA.

WILLIAMS, WHITE & CO.
MANUFACTURERS OF THE

Best Drop Hammer, with Crank Lift, in America.

Also a Machine for BENDING IRON into almost any shape with accuracy and dispatch — of great utility to Plow-Makers, Car-Builders, and Iron Safe Manufacturers. Also a superior GANG BORING MACHINE, running from four to eight spindles and bits at once, usually six — one man thereby doing the work of six. Also JUSTICE PATENT POWER HAMMER, Lever Trip Hammers, Power Punch and Shears, Upright Drills; Machine for Bending Staples, very accurate and rapid, and Wood-Shaping Machines. Also Steam Engines, and a full line of Saw-Mill Machinery and Steel and Iron Shafting, Hangers, Mill Gearing, and Heavy Castings and Forgings.

MOLINE, ILLINOIS.

GEORGE R. MARVIN,

Davenport Shirt Factory
AND
STEAM LAUNDRY.

Anchor Shirts.   Large Collars Made to Order.

225 Perry St. Davenport, Iowa.

B. F. TAYLOR,
MANUFACTURER OF
FINE CANDIES
WHOLESALE AND RETAIL.

Finest Ice Cream and Oyster Parlors in the City.

210 BRADY STREET,   DAVENPORT, IOWA.

SMITH & McCULLOUGH,
MANUFACTURERS OF AND DEALERS IN
Furniture, Carpets, Mattings,
LACE CURTAINS, DRAPERY, SHADES, ETC.

Agents for Andrews' Parlor Folding Beds, The Novelty Bed Lounge, and Marks' Adjustable Chair.

112 and 114 East Second St.   DAVENPORT, IOWA.

G. M. SCHMIDT,
DEALER IN
BOOTS AND SHOES
Ladies' and Gentlemen's Fine Shoes a Specialty.

Southwest Cor. Harrison and Second Sts.   DAVENPORT, IOWA.

H. H. ANDRESEN, Pres.   ROBT. KRAUSE, Sec.   L. P. BEST, Supt.

Davenport Glucose Mfg. Co.
SUPERIOR DOUBLE-REFINED
Grape Sugar, Glucose and Table Syrups,
DAVENPORT, IOWA.

WM. THOMPSON,
DEALER IN
Groceries, Fruits, Vegetables,
OYSTERS, FISH, SMOKED MEATS, ETC.

Goods delivered free to any part of city.

405 BRADY STREET,   **DAVENPORT, IOWA.**

BUY THE BEST—THE DAVENPORT CRACKERS.

REUPKE, SCHMIDT & CO.
MANUFACTURERS OF ALL KINDS OF
FINE CRACKERS

Capacity, Ninety Barrels Flour Per Day.

Office and Factory:
Cor. Fourth and Iowa Sts.   **DAVENPORT, IOWA.**

Orders by Mail promptly attended to.

W. W. Kimball's Branch House,
1726 Second Avenue,   Rock Island, Illinois.

Hallett & Davis Pianos, Emerson Pianos, W. W. Kimball Pianos,
In New Designs, Grand, Upright, and Square.

Turns Out Forty Finished Organs Per Day.

N. B. Our Factory, corner of 26th and Rockwell Streets, CHICAGO.

W. W. Kimball Organs.

TELEPHONE 54.
Wholesale and Retail Depot for **PIANOS & ORGANS**

ADDRESS
D. ROY BOWLBY,
Manager.

Geo. W. Cable, President. J. A. Freeman, Secretary.

CABLE LUMBER CO.
Steam Gang Saw Mills

BRIDGE TIMBER A SPECIALTY.

DAVENPORT, IOWA.

R. BENTON. C. H. BENTON.

BENTON'S
Livery, Sale and Feed Stables,

R. BENTON & SON,

Cor. Third and Rock Island Sts.   DAVENPORT, IOWA.

Horses Bought, Sold, and Exchanged.

ISAAC ROTHSCHILD,
LEADING
Clothier and Merchant Tailor,

DEALER IN

GENTS' FURNISHING GOODS, HATS, CAPS & TRUNKS,

Cor. Second and Brady Sts.   DAVENPORT, IOWA.

BERWALD & FRISIUS,

IMPORTERS OF AND JOBBERS IN

Toys, Stationery, Fancy Goods

Druggists' Sundries, Musical Instruments, Violin Strings, Etc.

214 WEST SECOND STREET,   DAVENPORT, IOWA.
Between Harrison and Main.

C. S. ELLS, President.   C. W. HEALD, Vice-President.
W. T. BALL, Secretary.

Union Malleable Iron Company,

MOLINE, ILL.

MANUFACTURERS OF

→Malleable Iron Castings←

OF EVERY DESCRIPTION.

SEND FOR CATALOGUE.

Moline Wagon Company

MOLINE,   ILLINOIS.

MANUFACTURE THE BEST GRADES ONLY.   MANUFACTURE THE BEST GRADES ONLY.

FARM AND SPRING WAGONS.

Capacity, Over One Hundred Wagons Per Day.

Illustrated Catalogue Mailed Free, on Application.

CONTENTS.

		PAGE.
CHAPTER	I. — By Way of Explanation,	17
CHAPTER	II. — A Glance Backward,	18
CHAPTER	III. — Location and Population,	19
CHAPTER	IV. — The Island of Rock Island,	20
CHAPTER	V. — Fort Armstrong — The Island, 1804-62,	22
CHAPTER	VI. — General Rodman's Work and Death.	23
CHAPTER	VII. — Colonel Flagler's Command,	25
CHAPTER	VIII. — Arsenal and Armory Shops,	26
CHAPTER	IX. — The Island Bridges,	27
CHAPTER	X. — Design of the Arsenal,	29
CHAPTER	XI. — The Island as a Conservatory of Birds.	30
CHAPTER	XII. — Island Incidents,	32
CHAPTER	XIII. — Davenport,	35
CHAPTER	XIV. — Rock Island.	36
CHAPTER	XV. — Moline,	37
CHAPTER	XVI. — The Great Water Power,	38
CHAPTER	XVII. — Manufacturing Advantages,	42
CHAPTER	XVIII. — Diversity of Resources,	44
CHAPTER	XIX. — Transportation Facilities.	45
CHAPTER	XX. — The Hennepin Canal.	48
CHAPTER	XXI. — Means of Communication.	50
CHAPTER	XXII. — Banking Houses,	52
CHAPTER	XXIII. — Factories and Mills.	53
CHAPTER	XXIV. — The Jobbing Trade,	55
CHAPTER	XXV. — The Press.	56
CHAPTER	XXVI. — Educational Advantages,	57
CHAPTER	XXVII. — The Public Schools,	58
CHAPTER	XXVIII. — Free Public Libraries,	59
CHAPTER	XXIX. — Hotels and Opera Houses.	61
CHAPTER	XXX. — Notable Institutions,	62
CHAPTER	XXXI. — Churches and Societies,	65
CHAPTER	XXXII. — Business Associations.	66
CHAPTER	XXXIII. — Black Hawk's Watch-Tower,	67
CHAPTER	XXXIV. — Meteorological Summary.	70

LIST OF ILLUSTRATIONS.

	PAGE.
Map of the Island of Rock Island,	Frontispiece
Black Hawk,	18
Main Entrance to Arsenal,	20
General Rodman,	23
Colonel D. W. Flagler,	25
Partial View of Armory Shops,	26
Soldiers' Barracks,	29
Colonel George Davenport,	32
Colonel Davenport's House in 1860,	33
General Rodman's Tomb,	34
View of Slyvan Water opposite Moline,	38
Arsenal Water-Power Machinery,	40
Arsenal Gun Yard,	43
Railroad Bridge Across the Mississippi River,	46
Map of the Proposed Hennepin Canal,	49
Rock Island and Davenport Ferry,	50
Colonel Flagler's Home,	51
Armory Rolling-Mill Chimney,	53
Cook's Home for the Friendless,	63
Armory and Arsenal Shops when in Process of Erection,	64
Grace Cathedral, Davenport,	65
Black Hawk's Watch-Tower, looking east,	68
Black Hawk's Watch-Tower (front view),	69

THE Chicago, Rock Island & Pacific
——— RAILWAY ———
IS THE DIRECT ROUTE FROM
✦ CHICAGO ✦
— TO —
Moline, Davenport, and Rock Island
Affording People from or to the East Unexcelled Accommodations and Facilities.

FIVE PASSENGER TRAINS DAILY,
——— EQUIPPED WITH ALL MODERN IMPROVEMENTS. ———

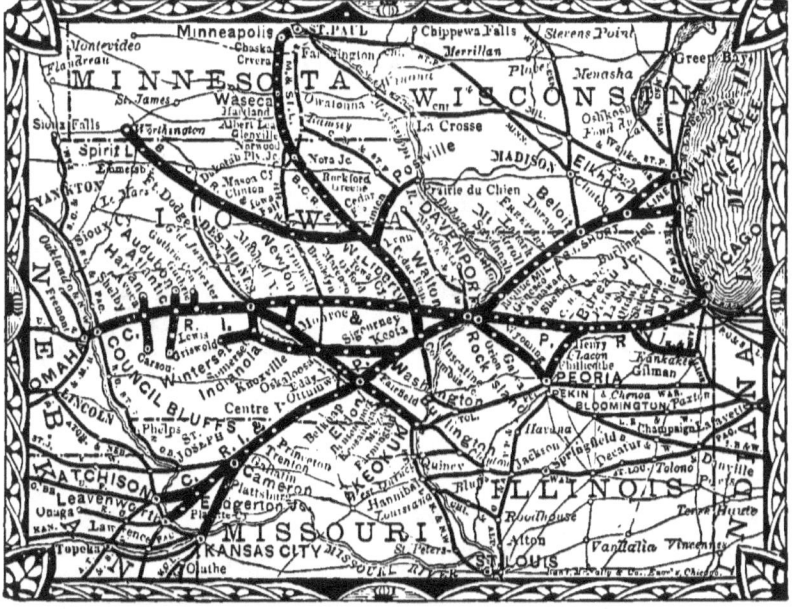

THE GREAT ROCK ISLAND ROUTE
CONNECTS THE EAST WITH THE GREAT CITIES OF
Kansas City, Leavenworth, Atchison, Council Bluffs, and Des Moines,
AND, BY ITS ADJUNCT, THE
ALBERT LEA ROUTE
With Minneapolis and St. Paul.

Fare always as low as the lowest. Through Tickets and Baggage checked to destination.

R. R. CABLE,
President and Gen. Manager.

E. ST. JOHN,
Gen. Passenger and Ticket Agent.

—— ESTABLISHED 1865. ——

U. N. ROBERTS & CO.

—— *WHOLESALE* ——

GLAZED SASH,

MOULDINGS, BUILDING PAPER, &C.

We Furnish the **Best of Goods** at Lowest Possible Prices.

FACILITIES FOR SHIPPING TO ANY PART OF COUNTRY.

CORRESPONDENCE SOLICITED.

DAVENPORT, IOWA.

FIRST NATIONAL BANK,

DAVENPORT, IOWA.

THE FIRST NATIONAL BANK IN OPERATION IN THE UNITED STATES.

CAPITAL, ... $100,000   SURPLUS, ... $50,000
UNDIVIDED PROFITS, . . $50,000.

OFFICERS.

JAS. THOMPSON, Pres.   J. E. STEVENSON, V.-Pres.   JOHN B. FIDLAR, Cashier.

DIRECTORS.

WALKER ADAMS.	JAMES THOMPSON.	S. F. GILMAN.
HENRY W. KERKER.	A. BURDICK.	AUG. STEFFEN.
CHRIST. MUELLER.	J. E. STEVENSON.	NATHANIEL FRENCH.
	L. C. DESSAINT.	HENRY KOHRS.

A GENERAL BANKING BUSINESS TRANSACTED.

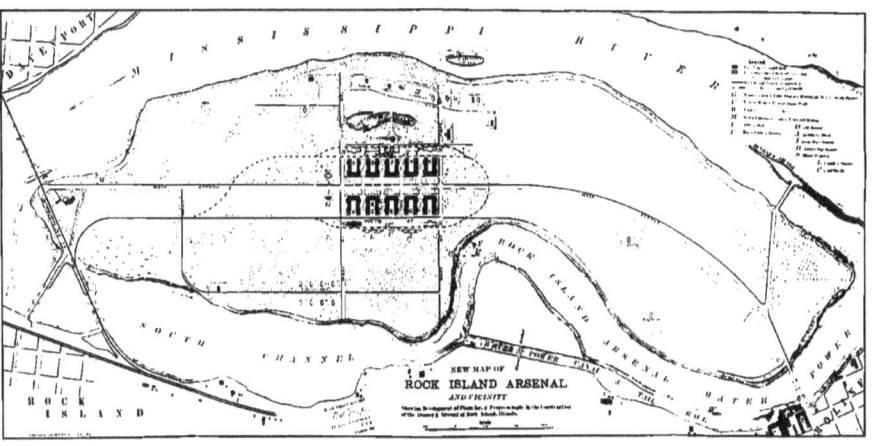

P

Three Cities,

AND THEIR

~~IN~~DUSTRIAL INTERESTS,

WITH AN

HISTORICAL AND DESCRIPTIVE SKETCH

OF THE

~~N~~ATIONAL ARMORY AND ARSENAL,

~~Lo~~cation, *Manufacturing Facilities, and Business Advantages*
~~of~~ Davenport, *Iowa, Rock Island and Moline, Illinois —
Their Trade and Commerce, Population, Schools,
Churches, and Present Condition.*

BY B. F. TILLINGHAST.

~~V~~alley of the Mississippi is, upon the whole, the most magnificent dwelling-place
~~b~~y God for Man's abode.—DE TOCQUEVILLE'S DEMOCRACY IN AMERICA.

DAVENPORT, IOWA:
GLASS & HOOVER, PRINTERS AND BINDERS.
1883.

INTRODUCTORY NOTE.

The special attention of readers is directed to the cards of business houses which appear in this book. They have been selected with the view of showing, together with the text, the extent, character, and diversity of the industrial interests, trade, and commerce of this manufacturing and jobbing center. Every firm, bank, factory, railroad, steamboat, professional, or other announcement, may be strictly relied upon. They represent lines of business thoroughly established and prosperous. Their names are but others for public spirit, enterprise, and liberal dealings.

COPYRIGHT,
1883,
BY B. F. TILLINGHAST.
ALL RIGHTS RESERVED.

CHAPTER I.

BY WAY OF EXPLANATION.

ALMOST daily for a period of ten years, the undersigned has been answering questions, as best he could, about Davenport, Rock Island, and Moline, their history, institutions, and industries. The inquiries have, like the ghost in the play, come in the most questionable shape, from transient visitors, press correspondents, and by letters from a distance. And, during the decade, the writer, in the pursuit of his business as the chronicler of local affairs, has exercised the utmost freedom in seeking information, only to repeat and scatter it. So it has naturally occurred to him to cover the ground once for all, in a series of pencil-pictures of the Tri-Cities, their location, resources, and enterprises.

The locality is certainly the most favored one in the Mississippi Valley. It is the site of the National Armory and Arsenal designed to be the greatest in the world. It is the manufacturing center of a vast and fertile country, covering inexhaustible beds of coal. Railroad lines diverge in all directions. Churches, colleges, academies, and school-houses are the monuments religion and intelligence have placed on every hand. Nature has been exceptionally generous in massing her gifts to delight the eye. Of all these, each in its turn, it is the object of these pages to speak.

No description, however vivid, could tell the whole truth about this interesting and picturesque locality. The eye of the artist and skill of the engraver have, therefore, been employed to supplement the story of the scribe. Without exception, all are new, and every illustration has been cut specially for use in this work. The writer takes pleasure in acknowledging the assistance, in this regard, of Mr. Henry Bosse, of Rock Island. To Colonel D. W. Flagler, commandant at Rock Island Arsenal, the writer's thanks are due for a revision of all matter pertaining to the Island, past and present; and to Captain R. R. Martin, Signal Service officer, for the full and valuable meteorological summary which appears at the close of the work. B. F. T.

CHAPTER II.

A GLANCE BACKWARD.

NEAR the center of the upper or northern half of the magnificent territory drained by the King of Rivers is the natural site of a populous city. Here was the chosen camping-ground of the Sac and Fox Indian tribes in the days of their power. It was the pride and glory of Black Hawk and his ancestors, and many are the records and legends of bloody warfare and romantic incident

BLACK HAWK.

associated with Indian life. It was in this vicinity that the old Sac warrior matured his plans to subdue his encroaching enemies, and here he fought his last battles to retain what he considered the garden-spot of the vast lands possessed by his tribe, and which he proudly spoke of as the earthly paradise of the Great Valley of the West.

But the contest proved unequal. The paleface pioneers came from Ohio, New York, and New England to occupy and possess the broad, rolling prairies, of which bright-colored but not unreal accounts had reached them. No point of settlement attracted attention earlier than this — a locality rich in its loveliness, fertility, and varied resources.

Thus "a local habitation" has been made within the memory of men whose allotted years have yet long to run. The last year, 1882, was the half-centennial of its history. At the close of the Black Hawk War, in 1832, there were no settlements on the Iowa side of the river. The purchase from the Indians of the territory now comprising Scott County was made, in common with all the river counties, on the 15th of September, 1832, the treaty having been made on the one side by General Scott. In the year following the tide of emigration began, in a feeble way, to flow in. Each succeeding year it grew larger, as it has continued to do without interruption since.

CHAPTER III.

LOCATION AND POPULATION.

THE object of this book is not to set forth the advantages or to enumerate the virtues of Davenport, on the west side of the river, or of Rock Island, Moline, and Milan, on the east side. It is to present as candidly as possible the attractions of the cluster of cities which form the setting for the gem of Mississippi River islands. The interests of all are the interests of each — commercially, socially, and generally — and as one populous center of industry they are here regarded.

The reader may turn to any map and place a pin upon a point whose longitude is 13 degrees and 37 minutes west of Washington, and whose latitude is 41 degrees and 30 minutes north. From this a circle whose radius is four miles may be described, and one has before him the exact geographical location of the three cities. Or, with reference to well-known places, it may be said that the point already fixed — the hub of the wheel whose rim is our convenient boundary — is, by rail, 181 miles west of Chicago and 316 east of Council Bluffs; by river, it is 332 miles north of St. Louis and 397 south of St. Paul. Milwaukee is 197 miles distant; Kansas City, 339; Peoria, 91; Des Moines, 177; Dubuque, 107; Burlington, 84.

The population of this already defined ring, whose circumference is twenty-five miles, is very close to 60,000 people, distributed as follows: Davenport, 30,000; Rock Island, 16,000; Moline, 13,000; Milan, 1,000.

CHAPTER IV.

THE ISLAND OF ROCK ISLAND.

MAIN ENTRANCE TO ARSENAL.

THE most beautiful of the many islands which divide the waters of the Mississippi River, from its source to its mouth, is Rock Island. It is the object of attention and praise from the thousands of tourists who go up and down the river from May to October. Viewed from the deck of a steamboat, it is a picture of grandeur which dwells upon the vision, while many a traveler by rail stops here for a day to enjoy its shady drives and broad avenues. It is a magnificent national park—one which the public is always free to enjoy. Its location is fortunate—almost midway between the head of navigation and the largest river city.

A book might be written about the interesting history of this beautiful island. It derives its name from the nature of its formation. The Island rests upon a bed of rock, consisting mainly of gray magnesian limestone, which in places crops out on the surface, but is generally covered with from one to eight feet of earth, principally loam and clay, though sometimes sand or gravel. The limestone is hard, strong, and durable, though it is never found in strata suitable for quarrying purposes.

The length of the Island is nearly two and three-fourths miles, and its width varies from one-fourth to three-fourths of a mile. It contains, above low-water mark, 970 acres. The course of the Mississippi, for some six miles, is nearly with the sun, and lengthwise the Island lies east and west. The surface of the Island is waving, yet not to any marked extent, and it is covered generally with sparse timber. On much of it, the first growth of timber has been removed, and is replaced by a second growth, mixed with some large old trees that remain. The native trees are principally oak, elm, ash, basswood, hickory, and walnut. The highest part of the Island is that occupied by the shops, all of it being from 17 to 23 feet above the highest stage of water. The other high grounds are generally from 14 to 20 feet above high water.

At best, no description can convey to the reader any adequate idea of the charms disclosed to the visitor. A day may be passed in following the roads which wind around the Island's contour; or, more inviting still, the sylvan drives which wander in their ways almost at the will of the pleasure-seeker. Variety is easily found, as the driver, without warning, is sure to be led to or across broad avenues, one of which runs nearly the length of the Island centrally east and west, and two others cross it north and south.

Throughout the spring and summer, the Island is the home of the feathered songsters of all kinds. An Audubon would find in its animated colors and caroling trees a paradise of enjoyment. The year round the gray squirrels hold high carnival as its undisputed possessors. Shooting and trapping are not allowed. Dogs are never seen on the Island. But, rich in natural beauty as Rock Island is, it has become famed chiefly as the site of the National Armory and Arsenal, which are next described.

CHAPTER V.

FORT ARMSTRONG—THE ISLAND FROM 1804 TO 1862.

THE United States acquired its title to Rock Island through a treaty which was made by William Henry Harrison, Governor and Superintendent of Indian Affairs for the Indian Territory and District of Louisiana, with certain chiefs of the Sac and Fox tribes of Indians, at St. Louis, Mo., in November, 1804. Black Hawk, the famous Indian hero of the Black Hawk War, was the principal chief of the Sacs, and did not sign the treaty, but held, during the War of 1812 and the Black Hawk War, that the treaty was not binding. Various other treaties were signed by other chiefs and warriors, but it is doubted if Black Hawk wrote his name to any of these, though the records conflict.

The island of Rock Island was not occupied by white men, and appears to have had no history, until the breaking out of the war with Great Britain, in 1812. The Indians occupied it unmolested, and it was their favorite hunting and fishing ground, and its beautiful scenery and rich woods made it a favorite resort for feasts and for the performance of religious and other ceremonies.

In September, 1815, the Eighth United States Infantry was sent from St. Louis to establish a fort upon the Island. Owing to the difficulties of travel, the troops first landed on the Island May 10th, 1816. Soon after was commenced the construction of the fort, named Fort Armstrong, in honor of the Secretary of War. Its location was the extreme northwest corner of the Island. The fort had an interior of four hundred feet square. The lower half of the walls was of stone, and the upper half of hewn timber. The fort was completed in 1817, and from that time to the breaking out of the Black Hawk War, in 1831, no unusual event is connected with it.

After the close of the war, there were no further hostilities with Indians. A garrison was maintained at Fort Armstrong till May 4th, 1836, when the fort was evacuated. General Street, Indian agent, had charge of the Island until 1838, when Colonel George

Davenport succeeded him, remaining in charge two years. In 1840 an ordnance depot was established at the fort, of which Captain Shoemaker had charge until 1845, when the stores were removed to St. Louis Arsenal. From 1845 till the act for establishing the Rock Island Arsenal was passed, in 1862, the Island was in the charge of a civil agent or custodian employed by the War Department, out of the control of which it never passed.

CHAPTER VI.

GENERAL RODMAN'S WORK AND DEATH.

AS early as September, 1841, Congress passed an act for a thorough examination of the whole western country, "for the purpose of selecting a suitable site on the western waters for the establishment of a National Armory." The resulting Board of Examiners gave Rock Island favorable mention in their report. Following this, the efforts of residents were persistent in behalf of the Island.

The act of Congress locating the National Arsenal on Rock Island was approved July 11th, 1862, and it appropriated for that purpose $100,000. This was the first action of Congress looking definitely to the construction of the Arsenal.

Ground for the first building— that now seen at the extreme west end of the Island — was broken September 1st, 1863. The cornerstone was laid April 20th, 1864. The tower of this building is supplied with one of the best clocks in the United States. It has a dial

THE LATE GENERAL RODMAN.

twelve feet in diameter on each of the four sides of the tower, and a striking bell weighing 3,500 pounds. The dials can be easily read from the cities of Davenport and Rock Island.

General Thomas J. Rodman, the inventor of the famous gun bearing his name, was assigned to the command of the Arsenal in June, 1865, succeeding Major Kingsbury, who was the first ordnance officer in command. General Rodman assumed his duties August 3d, 1865, and his command continued until his death, June 7th, 1871. The assignment of this office was the strongest evidence possible that the Ordnance Department had fully determined to build here one of its large, if not its largest, arsenals.

It was on February 7th, 1866, that General Rodman submitted plans to the Chief of Ordnance, comprehending ten great shops, in two rows of five shops each, those on the north being designed for the Armory, and those on the south for the Arsenal. These plans were approved, and General Rodman began the execution of his mighty work.

An act of Congress approved March 3d, 1869, appropriated $500,000 for the construction of the bridge across the Mississippi. Upon this work of engineering General Rodman bestowed a great deal of time, labor, and trouble; and to him belongs the honor of completing the plans. He lived to see his plans for the Arsenal materialized in the construction of two of the great shops and the quarters for the commanding officer.

General Rodman died at his quarters at the Arsenal June 7th, 1871. At the request of the Chief of Ordnance, he was buried upon the Island, in a lot of ground set apart for that purpose, near the National Cemetery, at the east end of the Island. There a modest shaft, bearing the honored name of "RODMAN," marks the last resting-place of the illustrious soldier and noble citizen.

CHAPTER VII.

COL. FLAGLER'S COMMAND — REVIEW OF THE WORK ACCOMPLISHED.

COL. D. W. FLAGLER.

COL. D. W. FLAGLER was placed in command of the Arsenal by an order issued from the Adjutant-General's office, June 15th, 1871. His selection was one of great wisdom and appropriateness. It is gravely doubted if from the affluent list of ordnance officers another choice of equal aptness could have been made for the place. The interval of time (twelve years) demonstrates the sagacity of the assignment.

Colonel Flagler at once fully comprehended the importance of the great work placed in his charge, and to it he has since given his time, careful attention, and profound study. The plans, as he received them, were imperfect in the details compared with the elaborate work that has grown from them, with the numerous changes and improvements that have been made. Inventions of practical value, resulting in conceded economy, have been applied. The progress of construction has been supplemented by the manufacture of stores for the army to the extent of $125,000 annually. In this way, the Commandant has proved that ordnance stores can be manufactured here and distributed to the army cheaper than they can be fabricated in the east and brought west.

It would require pages where lines can be used to enumerate the works which have been begun, finished, or are now in course of completion, by Colonel Flagler. A glance over the field shows it to contain eight shops entirely built, the last two now being so far advanced as to be fairly included; the commanding officer's quarters; buildings for officers' quarters; the soldiers' barracks; post buildings; a complete system of sewers; the Moline bridge; roads, streets, and avenues about the Island; the water-power wall; powder magazine; pump house; the water-power improvement; transmission of power; the grading and ornamentation of grounds; the work of care and preservation of property; operating the drawbridge; excavations for an artificial lake; elevated water tank and system of water mains; the manufacture of shop fixtures and machinery. These, in part, furnish the reader an idea of the diversity of the vast national plant.

CHAPTER VIII.

ARSENAL AND ARMORY SHOPS—THEIR EXTENT AND CHARACTER.

PARTIAL VIEW OF ARMORY SHOPS.

THE row of five shops south of the main avenue are for the Arsenal, and the five north of the same avenue are for the Armory. The center shop in the row is the forging shop and foundry of the Arsenal, and the other four are designed for finishing, wood, leather, and metal-working shops of all kinds, for the manufacture of all the material of war. The center shop of the north row is the rolling mill and forging shop for the Armory, and the two on either side of it are finishing and wood-working, or "stocking," shops, for the manufacture of all kinds of small arms. The center shop in each row is only one story high, and the other four have a basement and three stories. The ground plans of all the ten shops are alike. Each building consists of two parallel wings, 60 by 300 feet, 90 feet apart. This leaves an interior court 90 by 238 feet. The porticoes at the sides project twelve feet, and are sixty feet wide, and those in front project two feet, and are also sixty feet wide. The total area of each shop, including thickness of walls, is 44,280 square feet — a little more than one acre.

The walls of all these buildings are entirely of stone. The exterior or face stones are heavy ashlar, laid in courses, jointed, and having a squarely-broken face, without tool-marks. The backing is rubble, laid also in courses, and has its face, which forms the interior of the wall, well pointed. The average thickness of the walls is as follows: First story, three feet four inches; second story, two feet ten inches; third story, two feet four inches. The amount of material entering into the construction of one of these buildings is enormous. In shop A, the first built, for instance, there are 30,115,800 pounds of rock; 26,000 of copper; 362,500 of slate; 1,331,500 of lumber; 2,199,646 of iron; 3,132,800 of brick; 200,000 of plaster.

CHAPTER IX.

THE ISLAND BRIDGES—ONE LEADING TO EACH OF THREE CITIES.

THE Island is connected with the Iowa side of the river by one bridge, and with the Illinois side by two bridges. The main bridge is at the extreme northwest corner of the Island. This spans the main channel of the Mississippi, and is the most sightly structure crossing the Father of Waters, with the exception of the great bridge at St. Louis. It is also one of the strongest and best built bridges in the United States. The total length of the bridge is 1,550 feet and 6 inches, divided into five spans and one draw, as follows: Beginning at the north end, the first span is 260 feet long; the second, third, and fourth are each 220 feet long; the fifth, 260 feet and 6 inches; and the total length of the draw is 368 feet. There is also a shore span at each end, to carry the railroad over the approaches to the wagon road. The span at the north, or Davenport, end is 197 feet long, and the one at the south, or Island, end is 100 feet and 8 inches long, making the total length of the bridge, including the shore spans, 1,848 feet and 2 inches. The draw is double, rests on a center pier, and gives, when open, clear water ways between the draw pier and the adjacent north pier on one side of the draw pier, and south abutment on the other side, of 162 feet each.

The superstructure of the main bridge is a double-system Whipple truss, with vertical main posts, and has two decks. The wagon road is on the lower, and the railroad on the upper, deck. The clear height between the wagon road and the upper deck is 12 feet and 6 inches, and the clear height between the rails of the railroad and the top bracing is 17 feet.

The travel over this bridge is constant, and that it is immense is shown by the record for the year ending December 31st, 1882. This gives the number of pedestrians crossing north as 265,942, and south as 268,116. The number of teams crossing north was 166,850, and south 165,631. This is exclusive of cars and engines, there being 21,023 passenger and 209,438 freight cars, and 14,420 locomotives, both ways.

At the southwest limit of the Island, there is a wagon bridge leading to the city of Rock Island. This is 600 feet in length, of four equal spans. The wagon way is 22 feet wide in the clear, and there are foot walks outside the chords, one on each side, six feet wide.

At its eastern or upper end, a bridge thrown across the south branch, known as Sylvan Water, connects the Island with the city of Moline. The length of this bridge is 711 feet. It has five equal spans, of 142 feet each.

CHAPTER X.

DESIGN OF THE ARSENAL.—"IN TIME OF PEACE PREPARE FOR WAR."

SOLDIERS' BARRACKS.

IT must be admitted that we should have a national defense. This granted, it is easy to show the necessity for building the Arsenal, and the economy to the United States in doing so. The Ordnance Department supplies the army with every article used by the soldier for offensive and defensive purposes. This embraces small arms; equipments for infantry, cavalry, and artillery; all ammunition of every kind for cannon, rifles, carbines, and pistols, and also fireworks (such as rockets); all cannon and gun carriages for field, siege, garrison, and mountain or prairie service; and all equipments for the last, which embrace harness, tools, implements, battery wagons, and forges. Of what has been named, everything will be manufactured at this Arsenal, except cannon and gunpowder, and probably one or both of these eventually. It was learned, in the late civil strife, that the material of war—everything the soldier fights with—should be manufactured in government shops, and that the government shops were inadequate for the work. They had about one-fifth of the capacity required for the first three years of the war.

It is proposed to make this Arsenal the Arsenal for the whole Mississippi Valley. When completed, if crowded to its full capacity in time of war, it will be sufficient to arm, equip, and supply an army of 750,000 men. The capacity of this Arsenal will be, finally —so it is estimated—two and one-half to three times that of all the arsenals the United States had during the war, and fully equal to all the necessities for the Northwest and the Mississippi Valley, from the Alleghanies to the Rockies.

CHAPTER XI.

THE ISLAND AS A CONSERVATORY OF BIRDS.

THE following letter, addressed to the author of this work by Colonel D. W. Flagler, grew out of an interview on the subject discussed:

ROCK ISLAND ARSENAL, July 16th, 1883.

DEAR SIR:—In reply to your inquiry in regard to the birds on the Island, I would state that I have always taken great pains to preserve and protect from molestation every variety of American bird found here. The result is, that not only the number of birds has greatly increased, but also many new varieties have come to the Island during the past ten years. I think many people would be astonished upon being informed of the number of varieties now on the Island.

Some years ago, my children made a study of these birds, and found no less than fifty-one different varieties here. As they certainly did not find them all, and as some new birds have come here since they prepared their list, I think the number may now be safely put at eighty, and nearly all of these are singing birds. I will give a copy of their list as they made it. It does not give scientific names, and contains errors; still, I think it may be interesting and useful to many persons desiring information on this subject.

GAME BIRDS.

Quail, or Bob White.	Snipe.	Plover.
Pheasant.	Woodcock.	Rail.

WOODPECKERS.

Sap-sucker.	Red-headed Woodpecker.	Flicker, or Yellow-hammer.

HAWKS.

Night-hawk.	Hen-hawk.	Sparrow-hawk.

SWALLOWS.

Rock Swallow.	River Swallow.	Mud Swallow.

MISCELLANEOUS.

Chippy.	Snow-bird.	Screech-owl.
Sparrow.	Blue-bird.	Great Horn-owl.
Red-eyed Fly-catcher.	Kingfisher.	Cat-bird.
Bee-bird.	Sand-martin.	Red-winged Black-bird.
Humming-bird.	House-martin.	Swamp Black-bird.
House Wren.	Orchard Oriole.	Whip-poor-will.
Linnet (three varieties).	Baltimore Oriole.	King-bird.
Indigo-bird.	Blue-jay.	Robin.
Bittern.	Rose-breasted Grossbeak.	Cuckoo.
Phebe-bird.	Scarlet Tanager.	Turtle-dove.
Red-bird.	Brown Thrush.	Yellow-bird.
	Wood Thrush.	

All of the above, except the snipe and snow-bird, nest and raise their young on the Island. Beside these, most of the western water fowl visit the shores of the Island during the year.

I desire to call your attention to the great importance, in my opinion, of the Island as a conservatory for these birds. Dense woodlands are sparse in this part of the country, and wherever they occur the march of improvement clears them away, and in this and many other ways our birds are disturbed, driven off, or destroyed. Many species are likely to become extinct, or, at least, to disappear from this part of the country.

The Island contains several varieties of woodland. Some parts of the low, swampy ground are preserved in dense, tangled, natural thickets, undisturbed by anyone, and will probably always be so. The Island being a permanent military post, under strict control, and likely to remain so as long as the country lasts, there is no reason why it should not remain a permanent and safe harbor and conservatory for our birds — at any rate, as long as the country remains. This is a matter of some importance, not only to the ornithologist, but to the general public.

I believe the public is now generally apprised of the fact that in our eastern cities, where English sparrows have been introduced, they have driven many varieties of our American birds from the parks. I know this has occurred in some of our eastern arsenals, and, lest it should occur here, I have tried, by shooting and in other ways, to prevent these sparrows from coming to the Island from the adjoining cities.

D. W. FLAGLER,
Lt.-Col. of Ordnance, Commanding.

CHAPTER XII.

ISLAND INCIDENTS.

Death of Colonel Davenport.

COLONEL GEORGE DAVENPORT.

COL. GEO. DAVENPORT, after whom the city of Davenport was named, was the first white settler at or in the vicinity of Rock Island, and afterward became Indian agent for the government and received a grant of land on the Island. His remarkable career is intimately connected with the history of the Island.

On the 4th of July,

COLONEL DAVENPORT'S HOUSE IN 1860.

1845, Colonel Davenport was brutally murdered in his own house, the family being absent at the time, at a picnic. This house is a landmark, and the subject of illustration. The murderers escaped unrecognized, but were afterward detected, and three of them — Aaron Long, John Long, and Granville Young — were executed on the 19th of the succeeding October. The skeleton of one of the Longs now does duty in the hospital museum. The house in which Colonel Davenport lived is still preserved, as one of the relics of the Arsenal. It is on the north side, and about one-half mile from the lower end of the Island.

The Indians' Guardian Spirit.

When the Indian chief Black Hawk discovered that troops had arrived on the Island, and that their purpose was to build a fort, he mourned, for, as he said, "This Island was the best one on the Mississippi, and had long been the resort of our young people during the summer. It was our garden, like the white people have near their big villages, which supplied us with strawberries, blackberries, gooseberries, plums, apples, and nuts of different kinds. Being situated at the foot of the rapids, its waters supplied us with the finest fish. In my early life, I spent many happy days on this Island. A good spirit had charge it, which lived in a cave in the rocks immediately under the place where the fort now stands. [At the present time this cave is to be seen in times of low water, at the extreme northwestern point of the Island.] This guardian spirit has often been seen by our people. It was white, with large wings like a swan's, but ten times larger. We were particular not to make much noise in that part of the Island which it inhabited, for fear of disturbing it, but the noise at the fort [old Fort Armstrong is referred to] has since driven it away, and no doubt a bad spirit has taken its place."

The Island During the War.

During the civil war, Rock Island was transformed into a military prison. From 1863 until the close of the war, there were upwards of twelve thousand Confederate soldiers confined as prisoners there. During that period the number of deaths was one thousand nine hundred and sixty-one, all the interments being made on the Island. The city of the dead so populated is no longer pointed out by the small mound or leaning headstone. These have all been leveled, and suggestions of the prison days are undisclosed.

GENERAL RODMAN'S TOMB.

The National Cemetery.

In the National Cemetery, at the upper end of the Island, lie the remains of about four hundred Union soldiers. The grounds are scrupulously cared for, and with each recurring 30th of May the graves are strewn with wreaths of flowers.

Colonel Flagler's History.

But the scope of this work does not permit further details of this enticing subject. An elaborate history of the Armory and Arsenal, replete with interesting incidents connected with the early Indian treaties, has been written by Colonel Flagler, and was published by the War Department in 1877. It is a work of nearly five hundred large pages, with numerous maps and plates. Visitors wishing to form a more intimate acquaintance with the national work herein sketched are invited to consult Colonel Flagler's volume, to be found at the public library in each of the three cities.

CHAPTER XIII.

DAVENPORT.

DAVENPORT is the metropolis of Iowa, excelling all other cities in the state in the picturesque beauty of its location. Approaching the city by rail from the east, or from the north or south by boat, the observer has his attention fixed upon the waving bluffs which follow the river east and west. Between the line of these and the river is a triangular-shaped plateau, narrowing at the eastern limits of the city, and large enough to accommodate a population of one hundred and fifty thousand. Handsome homes dot the bluffs, while much of the residence part of the city lies beyond, or to the north. River views, as building sites, have been largely occupied, the scope of country brought within the range of the eye furnishing variety of scenery unequalled. The drainage is naturally good, street rising above street like terraces. The city's growth has been mainly since 1850. Surrounded, as it is, by as rich a country as the rains of heaven fertilize, with every advantage offered to residents, the best sanitary conditions, pure water, cheap fuel, it invites capital and labor to utilize its splendid opportunities.

Davenport's bonded indebtedness is small, and the rate of taxation low. The corporation affairs rest with the City Council. The city is provided with 242 fire hydrants, for which it pays $70 each annually to the Water Company. The water works are unequalled in the West for their efficiency, and are connected with 26 miles of distributing mains. The city has a splendidly organized paid fire department in connection with the Gamewell Electric Fire Alarm of 24 stations. At night the streets are lighted by 217 gas and 162 oil lamps. The police regulations are strict, insuring good order and safety to property at all times. The sanitary condition is carefully looked after by a Board of Health. The death rate for several years past, in comparison with other American cities of similar size, was strikingly low.

CHAPTER XIV.

ROCK ISLAND.

ROCK ISLAND is one of the best-known cities in the West, its business for many years having been large. Giving its name to a leading railroad, it has been carried far and wide. It possesses the elements of prosperity, and the enterprise to use them. Its growth has been steady, every gain made being held. The location of the city is in the center of a fertile agricultural and productive mineral country. It is at the western extremity of the Island, on the Illinois side. South of the level plain upon which the city rests, the scene is broken by wooded bluffs, affording many a sloping lawn.

Rock Island has long been noted for its good government and the wise administration of its municipal affairs. These are regulated by a Council of ten Aldermen and the Mayor. The city has a well-drilled volunteer fire department of 110 men, divided into five companies, fully equipped. The city owns its water works, which were built in 1882 by the Holly Manufacturing Company, of Lockport, New York. They furnish an abundant supply of mid-channel water at all times, for fire and domestic uses. The number of gallons pumped in 1882 was 571,000,000. The out-door light is supplied by the tower system of electric illumination. This is supplemented in-doors by gas. There is a competent Board of Health, with ample powers, and an efficient police force. The streets are in a praiseworthy condition, and kept so. In brief, the municipal machinery is in perfect running order. The United States Engineer office, under charge of Captain A. Mackenzie, is located here. It has charge of the Mississippi River improvements from St. Paul to the mouth of the Illinois River. The amount appropriated last year was over half a million dollars for this work.

CHAPTER XV.

MOLINE.

MOLINE lies south of the eastern half of the Island, reaching westward to the limits of Rock Island and southward almost to Rock River, three miles distant, and whose confluence with the Mississippi is some six miles west. The site of the city is attractive and beautiful. The lower or plateau part is largely filled by factories, which occupy the river bank for more than a mile, being greatly advantaged by the fine water power to be maintained forever by the government. Moline is designated as the "Lowell of the West," and rightly, for it is one of the busiest, most thrifty cities in the country. Its bluffs and the plain stretching beyond them furnish the most desirable building room. As in the two cities already named, industry, sobriety, and enterprise are the marked characteristics.

Moline has a Common Council of ten members; a public library, started by subscription and maintained by tax; a fine fire department of four companies; a good system of water works; and gas for public and private lighting. Great attention is paid to maintaining good streets.

CHAPTER XVI.

THE GREAT WATER POWER.

VIEW OF SYLVAN WATER OPPOSITE MOLINE (WATER-POWER POOL).

THE three cities possess many remarkable advantages for economical manufacturing. In these days, when strife and competition are so sharp, only a very small advantage is necessary to determine the success of one locality, while another without such advantage is doomed to failure. The former gives its manufacturer an excess of profit, which increases and builds up his business; the latter gives a bare support, and when depression comes the manufacturer fails, and his business is given up.

One of the natural manufacturing advantages possessed by the three cities is a great water power, both developed and undeveloped, and this is not a small advantage. In proof of this is the fact that to-day there is not a successful cotton mill in the United States that has not a water power. The man who must buy coal to make his power has just that small drag upon him, in a close race, which permits his competitor to outstrip him and win.

The water power of the Rock Island rapids is almost unlimited. On it the United States Government has already constructed a water power of nearly four thousand horse power. The city of Moline owns one-fourth of this, and the right to lease so much of the remainder as the United States does not use in time of peace, when the Arsenal is idle. But this is a small matter compared with the power that is not yet utilized. In a distance of three miles, the whole Mississippi River flows down an incline of from seven to eight feet. To show that this power, if need be, can be grasped and put to work, a letter is copied from the commanding officer of the Rock Island Arsenal in answer to inquiries on the subject:

ROCK ISLAND ARSENAL, ILL.,
March 30th, 1883.

MESSRS. DEERE & Co., Moline, Ill. :

Sirs—Your letter of the 15th of February was received during my absence in California. I have given much attention to the subject of extending the water power wing dam across the river, both for the benefit of the water power and navigation, and have discussed the matter in reports to the Chief of Ordnance made several years ago.

It should be a low dam, so that it would not greatly impede the flow of the river and raise the river above it, except during low water, when this action is desirable. It should have an opening three hundred feet wide through it for the passage of rafts—and down boats, if they desire it—even at low water.

A canal with a lock, similar to the canal and lock at Keokuk, should be constructed along the Iowa shore, for the use of vessels during the time of low water. The wing dam would be so low that, in connection with the channel opening through it, it would not interfere with navigation in times of high water—that is, when there is enough water on the rapids below the wing dam for easy navigation.

First. It would be of great value to navigation on the rapids above the wing dam, and would probably give sufficient depth of water at the lowest stages nearly up to Le Claire.

Second. The benefit to navigation on the part of the rapids below the wing dam in enabling vessels to pass the rapids in all weather, at all times of the night, and by making the navigation perfect at all low stages of the river, would, in my judgment, warrant building the canal and lock.

Third. The capacity of the water power could be quadrupled by the improvement, and permit the use of such portion of the increased power as might be desirable along the Davenport shore.

If the Hennepin canal should enter the river at any point on the rapids above Rock Island, this improvement of navigation on the rapids, and particularly raising the water—that is, increasing its depth—in the river at the mouth of the canal, would be of the highest importance.

Very respectfully, your obedient servant,

D. W. FLAGLER,
Lt.-Col. of Ordnance, Commanding.

ARSENAL WATER-POWER MACHINERY.

The following data in regard to the power that would be obtained by such an improvement were obtained from Colonel Flagler in a personal interview. As stated by him, the figures given are only approximate, but are always within the mark. Of course there would be the least power at the time of extreme low water, when there is the least water. Estimates for power should, therefore, be based upon low water. As the river does not fall below a stage of two feet, except at intervals of many years, and then does not remain at this low stage but a short time, a stage of two feet is taken for a basis of calculation. (This stage of two feet means two feet on the gauge of the government bridge.) At this stage, the estimated flow of water in the Mississippi River is 47,000 cubic feet per second. If the wing dam were extended across the river, with an opening in it 200 feet wide, and the depth of channel at the opening were 6 feet, and the dam raised the water above it 2 feet, then the discharge of the opening would be about 12,200 cubic feet per second. Subtract this from the whole discharge of the river, and we have 34,800 cubic feet per second left for the water power.

The fall from the head of the wing dam to the foot of the Island, at a stage of 2 feet, is now, say, 7 feet and 9 inches. The dam would increase this to 9 feet and 9 inches. It would be safe, then, to assume an available head for water power at all the dams of $7\frac{1}{2}$ feet. With this head, the above water would give 27,650 horse power. About 6,500 horse power of this could be made available at Davenport, through a ship canal 400 feet wide, $5\frac{1}{3}$ feet deep, with a current of 2 miles per hour. This canal should be constructed by building a dyke about 400 feet from and parallel to the Davenport shore, the material for the dyke to be taken from the bottom of the canal. This dyke should be about 70 feet wide at bottom, 14 feet wide at top, 20 feet high at east end, 28 feet high at west end. The dyke and canal would cost about $250,000 per mile. This canal would give water enough both for navigation and the above amount of power, even at a 0 stage. The lock for the canal, if not a portion of the canal also, would be properly chargeable to the improvement of the river for navigation.

This short statement is intended to show, not only the amount of the immense power that is silently flowing past our doors, but also that it is feasible to capture this giant, harness him to our mills, and make him obedient to do our work. The figures show a total power of over 37,000 horse power. One-third of this utilized and rented at the very low rate of $20 per horse power per annum would produce an income of $250,000 per annum. It is certainly not saying too much when we say that if the American people ever require this power, they will take it and use it. If there are uses to which we can apply it, its value is too large a sum to be allowed to flow past our doors without picking it up.

CHAPTER XVII.

MANUFACTURING ADVANTAGES.

A QUESTION naturally suggested by the last chapter is, Shall we ever require this vast water power? If one may judge of the future by the past, there is every reason to expect it. During the past twelve years, the manufactures of the three cities (excepting lumber) have certainly quadrupled. The reasons or advantages which have caused this increase are very strong, and they still exist. Compared with eastern manufactures, some of these advantages are as follows:

First. We have now a large market in this region and further west for our manufactured goods. When ready for market, therefore, we save in price the freight from the East to this point.

Second. Most of our materials required for manufactures are here. The eastern manufacturer must transport them; or, at any rate, the price in the East is the price here plus the freight.

Third. The eastern manufacturer must transport from the West the food to feed his operatives. Generally, this advantage greatly outweighs both the others. Look at it how you will, the cost of an article manufactured in the East must include freight from the West on food to feed the workmen. The price of the food is its price in the West plus freight, plus the commission of half a dozen middlemen. Rents are also cheaper. The result is, that if this difference in price of bread, meat, and rent were taken from the eastern workman's wages, and only the remainder paid to the western workman, he would then be as well paid as at the East. The fact is, however, it is not all taken off. But a portion of it is, and the advantage is thus divided between the manufacturer and the workman; the manufacturer gets his labor for a less per diem, and yet the workman is better paid. It is this mutual advantage that causes both the manufacturers and workmen, mutually dependent upon each other, to seek out together localities advantageous to both.

The writer is told by Colonel Flagler, at the Arsenal, that this is exactly illustrated in his department. Eastern establishments doing precisely the same work that is done at Rock Island pay higher wages, yet the workmen are willing to come West. The same articles cost more manufactured in the East than at Rock Island, and the result is, the manufacture of more and more of these articles is being transferred by the War Department, each year, to Rock Island.

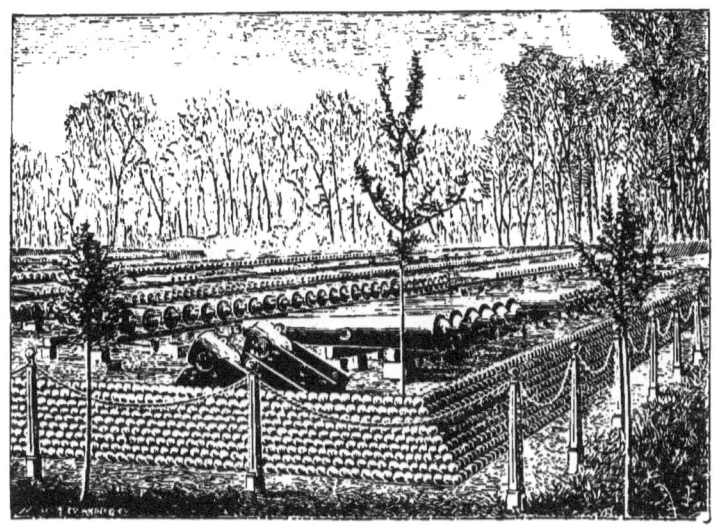

ARSENAL GUN YARD, ON MAIN AVENUE.

To illustrate the tendencies of manufactures, and of what has been said, let us take the case of manufactured cotton goods, and see if we may not even be sanguine enough to hope to have this great King Cotton among us some day. Starting at Memphis, one of the largest cotton markets, cotton is now taken by river to New Orleans, thence by vessel to New York, then to Boston, then to Lowell. At New Orleans it passes through the hands of two or three middle-men, and the same in New York. Beside the commissions of these middle-men, the wastage from sampling (it might sometimes be dignified with the name of stealing) is considerable. We then haul bread and meat from Illinois and Iowa to Lowell to feed the operatives. They manufacture the cotton into goods, and again it starts on its perilous journey amongst the middle-men, through Boston, New York, and Chicago, to Moline, Rock Island,

and Davenport. The average number of middle-men who have taken toll from the much-picked cotton between Memphis and Chicago is no less than seventeen. When we add the percentages and profits of all these gentlemen to the cost of this long, tortuous journey, and freight on the bread and meat, it foots up quite a respectable bill of *extras*.

Now, in comparison with this, let us estimate the saving of bringing this cotton direct from Memphis to this point, without middlemen, and sell it direct from the boat into the warehouse of a mill, where it finds a water power and cheap food for the operatives that are to spin it. When made up, it need go no further than Chicago to be sold; and though sold in Chicago, it can remain in the mill warehouse till shipped westward.

With all these advantages, in these times of sharp competition, is it unreasonable or audacious to expect that cotton and many other manufactures, if once started, might come here and demand a water power? If they get it, they will succeed, as others here have already done.

CHAPTER XVIII.

DIVERSITY OF RESOURCES.

THE central location of these cities, combined with the important natural advantages noticed in the preceding chapter, are some, rather than all, of the factors which must contribute to the material development. There are others as yet too briefly noted.

The wide country at the west, north, and south is fast filling up with an intelligent and enterprising people, who will become residents and tillers of the soil. They carry with them all the wants incident to high civilization. The whole region, for a thousand miles west of the Mississippi River, is, perhaps, a country of richer soil than is to be found elsewhere in the world. It is, in fact, an empire in itself. These wants will naturally be supplied where the commodity can be made and transported to the consumer most cheaply. In former, though still recent, times, manufactured commodities came from the older states, but now it is demonstrated that manufacturing can be done and the commodities furnished more economically than by buying from the older states.

Added to the vast water power, there are inexhaustible coal mines near at hand, the product of which, within a radius of fifteen miles, is 500,000 tons annually. The iron of Lake Superior and Missouri, together with that of Tennessee and Pennsylvania, furnish the raw material at a cost for transportation comparatively small. The pineries of the north furnish an abundance of soft woods for housebuilding. Of this the river floats to and by this locality each summer more than one thousand million feet. The great hard-wood forests of the southern states furnish all the material necessary to enter into the construction of farm machinery.

The history of manufactures in the West shows they have been chiefly directed to, and have been eminently successful in, the production of agricultural implements. Thus have been developed here the largest plow factories in the world. But the time is at hand for the making of textile fabrics of cotton and wool on a scale similarly magnificent.

CHAPTER XIX.

TRANSPORTATION FACILITIES.

ONE of the largest manufacturing houses of its class in the country was established in the Tri-Cities a year since, removed here from a distant point after an examination of the claims of ten western cities. There are greater railroad centers, but they are without the Mississippi River. From Davenport, Rock Island, and Moline, there are iron and water outlets north, south, east, and west, entering a country of phenomenal resources.

The commercial or other traveler has the means always at hand, through the railroads, of making an expeditious journey in any direction. After the day's business he may enter his moving bedroom, known as the sleeping-car, and, without further thought, awake in

RAILROAD BRIDGE SPANNING THE MISSISSIPPI OPPOSITE DAVENPORT.

the morning in Chicago, Milwaukee, St. Paul, Minneapolis, Council Bluffs, Kansas City, Leavenworth, St. Louis, or Indianapolis. Transacting twelve hours business, he may return home, having been absent from his desk, store, or shop but one day.

The Chicago, Rock Island & Pacific Railway has practically four divisions from as many directions meeting here — the Southwestern, the Main Line in Iowa, the Albert Lea, and the Illinois — with 1,700 miles of road. Its connections are close with a network of lines ramifying almost every county in the Northwest.

The Chicago, Milwaukee & St. Paul Railway has a total mileage of its own of 4,455 miles — the longest of any single corporation in the world. A car may be loaded in either of the three cities for any point upon this line or its connections.

The Chicago, Burlington & Quincy Railroad, another of the great trunk lines, with its 3,714 miles of track, competes for business here, and opens a vast territory reached only by itself.

The Rock Island & Peoria Railway is a short line, with connections for Indianapolis and Cincinnati.

The Coal Valley Mining Company's and the Rock Island & Mercer County lead to inexhaustible coal-fields.

The Davenport, Iowa & Dakota is a projected line to Dakota, for which the city of Davenport has given liberal franchises.

The Rock Island & Southwestern is another surveyed route to Kansas City.

Several miles of side-tracks have been built, each of the carrying corporations showing a liberal spirit in fostering trade, particularly manufacturing, along its line. Special advantages are given shippers in the way of side-track facilities, cars, rates, and accommodations.

Two lines of river steamers — the St. Louis & St. Paul Packet Company and the Diamond Jo Steamboat Line — with independent boats plying the river, afford competition for freights during the season of navigation.

CHAPTER XX.

THE HENNEPIN CANAL.

THIS favorably known link of water communication between the Mississippi River and Lake Michigan, thereby affording an all-water route to the seaboard, is an improvement of national importance, and has been so recognized by the Forty-seventh Congress. The building of this canal, now assured, is the solution, in a large measure, of the cheap transportation problem.

By the action of the General Assembly, sanctioned by the popular vote of Illinois, the Illinois & Michigan Canal, extending from Chicago to Hennepin, has been ceded to the United States. This has been done with the understanding that the general government will accept the grant and complete the canal (for which the surveys have been made) to a point on the river at or near Rock Island. The length of the unbuilt link is only sixty-five miles. With this water route opened to boats, the farmers and merchants, mechanics and manufacturers, of the whole Northwest, will be the gainers. These cities will not only share the common good fortune, but they will reap, inevitably, local benefits of no mean proportions.

The map on the opposite page conveys the whole subject to the eye at a glance. The cost, according to the estimate made by the War Department in 1870, will be $3,899,723. The Hennepin Canal is the grandest national work ever undertaken in the interest of cheap transportation. The seven northwestern states, whose commerce it will cheapen, produced, in 1879 (according to United States census), in round numbers, 1,300,000,000 bushels, or 70,000,000 tons, of grain alone. The saving of two cents a bushel on one-half of this amount would net $13,000,000 in one year, or enough to build three such canals.

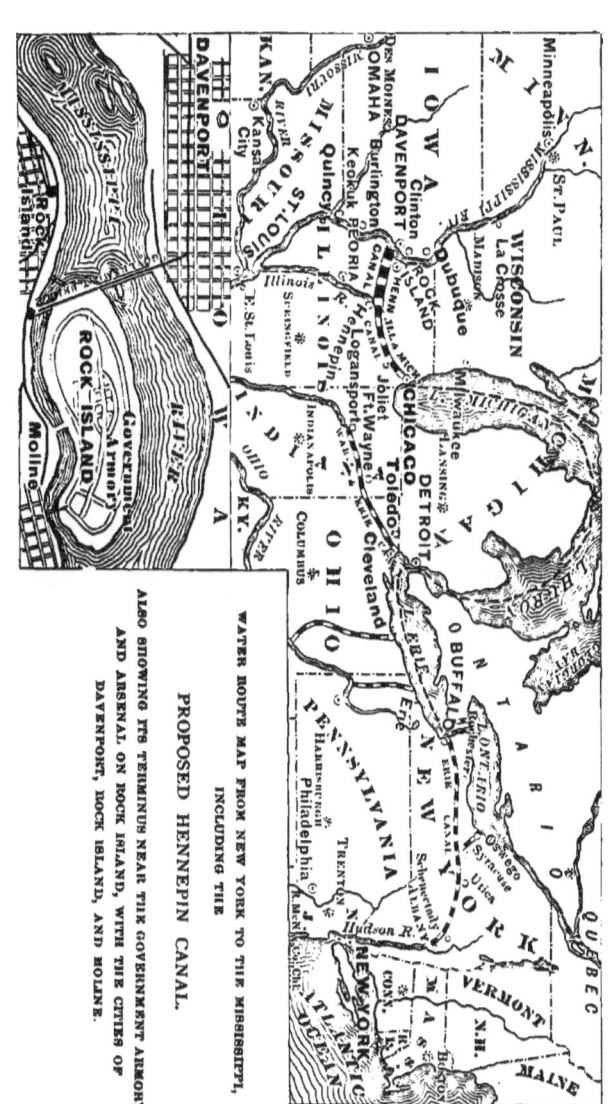

WATER ROUTE MAP FROM NEW YORK TO THE MISSISSIPPI, INCLUDING THE

PROPOSED HENNEPIN CANAL.

ALSO SHOWING ITS TERMINUS NEAR THE GOVERNMENT ARMORY AND ARSENAL ON ROCK ISLAND, WITH THE CITIES OF DAVENPORT, ROCK ISLAND, AND MOLINE.

CHAPTER XXI.

MEANS OF COMMUNICATION.

ROCK ISLAND AND DAVENPORT FERRY.

THIS book is written in the hope that it may fall into the hands of strangers, thousands of whom visit the locality in quest of pleasure or in search of business opportunities. These have at their command several means of transit between the places of interest, which will be described later. The visitor of a day or of a week will find his time only too brief, accordingly as he arranges for a superficial or a more systematic inquiry.

If but a single day is allotted, a carriage should be ordered, and all the better if an experienced driver is called for with it. A ride about Davenport, over the bluffs to the Soldiers' Orphans' Home, or to Linwood, a summer resort six miles down the river, with a stop here and there for views, will occupy a forenoon. Five hours more will hardly suffice for a hurried drive across the Island to Moline, through the main streets of that city of factories, and to the brow of the commanding bluffs. Continuing three miles south, the tourist will reach Rock River. Following the winding road four miles further, and the summit of Black Hawk's Tower, the highest point on the south side of the Mississippi, is gained. From this outlook the view is extended and beautiful, and the scenery inspiring. Three miles more complete the circuit to Rock Island city and consume the time, which will have been found only too short.

A more leisurely way — and the cheaper, too — is to use the street cars. These will give twelve miles of travel about Davenport, convey the sight-seer from the western limits of Rock Island to the eastern part of Moline, and from the central part of Rock Island to Black Hawk's Tower and to Milan. A fine ferry steamer makes trips across the river every fifteen minutes, and a free bridge is always at the pleasure of the pedestrian. Steam cars leave the depots in each city at convenient hours for either of the four places named.

The complete telephone system brings the four places within speaking distance of each other. The Exchange has a central office in each city, at which connection can be made with eight hundred business houses and residences, hotels, depots, etc.; also,

COLONEL FLAGLER'S HOME.

with more than fifty surrounding towns, within a range of one hundred miles, such as Clinton, Muscatine, Geneseo, Sterling, etc.

If the stranger desire to confine his visit to gathering information in one or two particular directions, as the factories, schools, or Arsenal, he will find those mentioned in separate chapters.

CHAPTER XXII.

BANKING HOUSES.

THE preceding pages have spoken of the locality as offering unequalled inducements to capital and for its profitable investment. It is now left to present the proof of this. Money is always seeking just such opportunities, and if they exist, they are sure to be found and put to the practical test. This has been done, and the result shows that the most extravagant claim made is within the truth. There is not a city of 60,000 people in the United States whose volume of business is larger, which rests upon a surer basis, whose industries are more varied, or whose prosperity is more genuine and placed farther beyond dispute. The commercial reports confirm the assertions made to a demonstration.

The banks are a true index of business transactions. There are twelve of these financial institutions doing business here — eight national, three savings banks, and one private banking house — divided as follows: The First National, Davenport National, Citizens National, German Savings, and Davenport Savings banks, in Davenport; the Rock Island National, First National, People's National, and Mitchell & Lynde's banks, in Rock Island; the First National, Moline National, and Moline Savings banks, in Moline.

According to the statements of the eight national banks recently made, their resources were $4,564,523.03. This is exclusive of private bank. The item of deposits in the nine banks at the time named amounted to $2,646,535.92. The amount of exchange drawn by the banks of the three cities for the year 1882, upon Chicago, St. Louis, and New York, was $57,354,520.

The foregoing takes no account of the savings banks. At the time designated, their depositors numbered 7,753, and the amount of their savings in bank were $3,411,338.20.

These figures tell their own story of industry, frugality, and thrift.

CHAPTER XXIII.

FACTORIES AND MILLS.

ARMORY ROLLING-MILL CHIMNEY.

IN extent, variety of industries, number and prosperity, no other western community can be favorably compared with this for its manufacturing resources. A bare enumeration must suffice where a much larger book would be required by even a partial description.

Moline.

In this city are operated Deere & Co.'s Plow Works; the Moline Plow Co.; J. S. Keator & Sons' and Dimock, Gould & Co.'s saw mills; the Union Malleable Iron Co. and the Moline Malleable Iron Works; Williams, White & Co.'s Iron Works; the Deere & Mansur Corn-Planter Works; Moline Scale Co.; Moline Elevator Co.; Schillinger & Trumble, boiler works; Moline Wagon Co.; the Moline Paper Co.; the Moline Pump Co.; the Moline Pump Works; the Moline Pipe Organ Co.; Colseth & Co., cabinet organs; Barnard & Leas Manufacturing Co.; Moline Road Cart Co.; Matteson Brothers, machine shops; Moline Stove Co.

Rock Island.

The Rock Island Plow Works of B. D. Buford & Co.; Weyerhauser & Denkmann's saw mill; the Rock Island Lumber and

Manufacturing Co.; Rock Island Stove Works; Rock Island Baby Carriage Works; J. M. Christy, cracker factory; John Volk & Co., sash and doors; George Wagner, I. Huber, Raibel & Stengel, breweries; Warnock & Ralston, soap and candles; J. S. Gilmore, pork packing; Carse & Ohlweiler and J. G. Junge, bottling works; Kahlke & Brothers, boat-ways; William Farrell, bone-meal factory; Crampton & Co., books and binding; William Gray, box factory; Kurth & Scherer, W. M. Wall, Willis & Brubaker, carriages; C. C. Knell, furniture; Downing Brothers and W. H. Thompson, foundries; Frank Ill and C. Churchill, wagons; L. Meese & Co., hosiery; Rock Island Glass Works; Kimball's Piano Factory; D. Donaldson, saw works.

Davenport.

The Eagle Manufacturing Co.; the Davenport Plow Co.; Lindsay & Phelps, Cable Lumber Co., Renwick, Shaw & Crossett, Schricker & Mueller, and Paige, Dixon & Co., saw mills; the Le Claire Foundry; Ebi & Neuman's Machine Shops; Grupe & Murray, boiler works; George H. Young & Co., J. L. Mason, A. Woeber, and A. C. Duve, carriage works; Davenport Pump Co.; the Smith & Stearns Paint Co.; the Davenport Woolen Mills; the Crescent, Farmers, and Phœnix flour mills; the Davenport Oat Meal Co.; Reupke, Schmidt & Co. and Eagle Co., cracker factories; U. N. Roberts & Co., T. W. McClelland & Co., Geo. Ott, Flexner & Smith, J. H. Whitaker, F. Ranzow & Son, sash, blind, and door factories; Koehler & Lange, M. Frahm, Lage & Co., J. G. Baumeier, breweries; N. Kuhnen, Otto Albrecht & Co., cigar factories; Davenport Glucose Works; Reimers & Fernald, candy; Ranzow & Haller, Henry Kohrs, J. L. Zoeckler, and John Ruch, pork-packers; Egbert, Fidlar & Chambers, books and binding; H. F. Moeller, box factory; Robert Krause, clothing; West Davenport Furniture Co.; Haight & Sears, horse collar factory; Davenport Ladder Co.; John Zimmerman, pianos; Davenport Pottery; Boudinot & Sons' Rope Walk; J. C. Bills & Co., show cases; S. R. Jones, spice mills; John S. Davis Sons, threshing machines; J. W. Wirtel, trunks; Amazon Vinegar Works; Davenport Steam Heating Co.; George R. Marvin, shirt factory.

Milan.

Milan Wagon Works; the Milan, National, and Rock Island Paper Companies; D. B. Sears & Sons and the Johnston flour mills; Graham Cotton Mills.

Manufacturing Statistics.

The following figures, which show the statistics of manufacturing in this locality, are, perhaps, more nearly correct than those obtained from any other source. But there should at least be added an increase of twenty-five per cent for the gain since the national census of June, 1880, was taken:

Number of establishments,	469
Capital invested,	$7,721,979
Males above 16 years employed,	4,777
Females above 15 years employed,	150
Children and youth,	482
Total wages paid in one year,	$2,305,320
Value of materials used,	$7,708,166
Value of products,	$12,461,779

CHAPTER XXIV.

THE JOBBING TRADE.

THE reader is doubtless prepared to accept, without question, the statement that there is no fictitious progress about the three cities. The elements of their stability and thrift are exposed to the view of every one. While the manufacturing interests are, perhaps, the leading ones, they do not dim the importance of the wholesale trade. The volume of this business transacted for the last calendar year was in excess of $10,000,000. The lines of business represented are the following:

Groceries and Provisions — Beiderbecke & Miller and Van Patten & Marks, Davenport; Henry Dart's Sons, Rock Island.

Tobacco and Cigars — N. Kuhnen, Otto Albrecht & Co., Davenport; C. H. Schocker, J. R. Johnston, Rock Island; R. Reimers, Moline.

Boots and Shoes — Bryant & Doe, Davenport.

Paper Stock — M. N. Nixon, Davenport.

Cloths and Clothing— Robert Krause, Davenport.

Crockery and Glassware— Jens Lorenzen, W. H. & C. T. Webb, Davenport; May Brothers, Rock Island.

Dry Goods— W. C. Wadsworth & Co., A. Steffen, J. H. C. Petersen & Sons, Davenport.

Hardware— Sickels, Preston & Co., L. C. Dessaint, Davenport; Stewart & Montgomery, Rock Island.

Iron and Wagon Stock— Sieg & Williams, Davenport.

Hides, Pelts, and Tallow— D. H. McDaneld, Davenport.

Paints, Varnish, Drugs, and Oils— Smith & Stearns Paint Co., Davenport; Hartz & Bahnsen, Rock Island.

Leather, Saddlery, etc.— Haight & Sears, Davenport; J. C. McConnell & Co., J. & M. Rosenfield, Rock Island.

Candy, Nuts, etc.— Reimers & Fernald, Davenport.

Sash, Doors, and Blinds— U. N. Roberts & Co., George Ott. Flexner & Smith, Davenport.

CHAPTER XXV.

THE PRESS.

THE newspaper press is the reflection of the people for whom it is published— their homes and hopes, institutions and interests. In it are mirrored the life and business, first of the locality, then of the world. These cities and this center may be well judged by their newspapers. They are loyal, enterprising, able, and jealous only of the good name and fair fame to which they have been ceaseless contributors. There are seven dailies, fourteen weeklies, one semi-weekly, and four monthlies, as follows:

Daily— Davenport Gazette, Davenport Democrat, Davenport Der Demokrat, Rock Island Union, Rock Island Argus, Moline Republican, Moline Dispatch.

The above-named papers all have weekly editions. There are, in addition, these weekly publications:

Weekly—Northwestern News, Davenport; Sternen Banner, Davenport; Dannebrog, Davenport; Herald, Davenport; Volks-Zeitung, Rock Island; Rock Islander, Rock Island; Citizen, Moline.

Monthly—Iowa Churchman, Davenport; Familien Journal, Davenport; Modern Miller, Moline; Western Plowman, Moline.

CHAPTER XXVI.

EDUCATIONAL ADVANTAGES.

A COMMUNITY may be correctly judged by its public schools and the advantages it offers for the advanced education of its youth. Singularly favored in these respects is this locality, whose colleges, academies, and graded schools are liberally sustained both by the general tax-payer and by private endowments. This system is progressive and broad; it invites the attention of the casual visitor and the inspection of the teacher.

Griswold College, Davenport, established and sustained under the auspices of the Episcopal Diocese of Iowa—William Stevens Perry, Bishop—occupies a crowning eminence in the central part of the city, overlooking the river scenery. The institution has a large endowment, which is being steadily increased. It has a library of more than 7,000 volumes. The faculty number eleven members. There are three departments—preparatory, collegiate (embracing scientific and classical courses), and theological. The curriculum is fully up to the highest standard. Griswold College has before it a bright future.

Augustana College and Theological Seminary, Rock Island, was chartered in 1865. It is under the exclusive control of the Swedish Lutheran Augustana Synod of the United States. The buildings have been erected at a cost of $50,000, and their site is a beautiful one. The library consists of over 10,000 volumes and pamphlets. The course of instruction has two departments—classical and scientific—each requiring four years. A special feature of the former is the attention paid to language studies. There are 150 students, nine professors, and two instructors.

Occupying ample grounds, with their terraced lawns, Davenport, is the Academy of the Immaculate Conception, now in its twenty-fourth year. It is conducted by the Sisters of Charity, and affords every facility for acquiring a thorough mental and moral education. The number of young ladies in attendance is about 160. The course includes music, painting, French, German, the Latin and English languages, and all the common academic studies.

St. Ambrose Seminary, Davenport, was opened by Bishop McMullen, in 1882, and now has about sixty pupils.

There are several parochial and other select or private schools, and two kindergartens. The Davenport Business College has an attendance varying with the season from 100 to 200 students.

CHAPTER XXVII.

THE PUBLIC SCHOOLS.

Davenport.

THE first school-house was built in Davenport in 1838, and the graded school system was organized in 1858. It has always been kept abreast of the rising generation. There are twelve school buildings, the largest of which is the High School, erected in 1874, at a cost, covering the grounds, of $65,000. The staff of instructors is composed of Superintendent J. B. Young, ten principals, and eighty teachers, ten of whom teach the German language. The enrollment and average attendance for 1882 were larger than ever before. The instructors have been so qualified for the work, that drawing and penmanship are successfully taught without the help of special teachers. The last census gave a school population of 9,523—boys, 4,592; girls, 4,931. The average number enrolled was 4,553, and the average attendance 3,527. The annual cost of the schools is $68,000. The management rests in a Board of Education of six members, two of whom are elected each year. A free night school is maintained during five winter months.

Rock Island.

The public schools of Rock Island use seven large houses. The Superintendent, S. S. Kemble, has been prominently identified with the cause of popular education here for seven years. Forty regular teachers are engaged, and one special instructor in music. The total enrollment, as given by the last report, was 2,233, and the average attendance 1,575. The school census gives the number between six and twenty-one years as 3,590. The cost of tuition for each pupil enrolled is $11.12, and few cities show so good returns for the money expended. The system is thoroughly graded, and the schools most efficiently conducted.

Moline.

The growth of Moline has been rapid—a fact attested by the frequent enlargement of its school facilities. It now has four buildings, three of which are noble structures of brick, eligibly located. The High School building is the most conspicuous in the city. Twenty-seven teachers are employed. Special instruction in vocal music is given. The superintendent is W. S. Mack, an educator of exceptional ability, who is now serving his fifth year. A free night school is maintained during the months of November, December, January, and February. The number of school age is 2,379, and the enrollment 1,787. The cost of tuition per pupil for the last year, 1882, based on the average monthly enrollment, was $10.80.

CHAPTER XXVIII.

FREE PUBLIC LIBRARIES.

ORDINARILY, bare mention would suffice, in a community whose active, growing years hardly number more than twenty-five, for the notice of those beneficent institutions, free public libraries. One expects to find them in the New England town, but does not look for them in many western cities. Not so here. Each of the trinity of cities has its free public library, and in no instance is it a struggling, empty-shelved nucleus unworthy the name.

Through the aid of a woman of blessed memory, Mrs. Clarissa C. Cook, a suitable building for a library, centrally located on Brady street, Davenport, has been erected, at a cost of $13,000, upon a lot bought with the proceeds of individual donations. It contains over 8,000 volumes of standard books. Upon the reading-tables are found the leading magazines and newspapers. The number of volumes drawn in 1882 was 8,730, and the number of visitors 10,908.

The Rock Island Public Library occupies pleasant rooms over the post-office. It was founded and is supported by the city. It is open to the public day and evening the year round—both the library proper and the reading-rooms. The last annual report of the Board of Directors, addressed to the City Council, has these words: "It is a source of gratification for us to know that the library is appreciated by the people. In their behalf, we thank you for your liberal appropriation." The amount referred to is $1,500. There are upon the shelves 6,800 volumes. The issue of books in 1882 was 19,705; the number of borrowers, 1,426; and the monthly average of attendance, 3,155.

The Moline Public Library was started in 1872 by a public subscription of $5,576, and opened June 6th, 1873. It occupies the two upper stories of the fine post-office building, donated forever for library purposes by S. W. Wheelock and wife. It has about 6,000 volumes of the best books, beside most of the current newspapers, periodicals, and magazines. It is a growing monument, attesting the intelligence of the people of the City of Mills. The annual revenue from municipal tax, rents, and subscriptions is $1,500. The circulation of books in 1882 was 13,412, and the average monthly attendance 1,990.

CHAPTER XXIX.

HOTELS AND OPERA HOUSES.

WHAT better index is there of a city's life and activity than the character of its hotels and the extent of their business? Many citizens live either temporarily or permanently at the hotels of these cities, while thousands of the traveling public make them transient homes. It is not an unusual day when the registers of the principal houses show four to five hundred arrivals. Every Sunday finds the commercial travelers gathered here to the capacity of the hotels, and they are the best authority for the statement that, outside of St. Louis and Chicago, there are to be found no such luxurious, homelike accommodations, or bills of fare so tempting. The facilities are large, as they must be for the demands made upon them, yet in times of state conventions or other large gatherings, the multitude is cared for.

The Kimball House, Davenport, is the largest and best hotel in Iowa, supplied with telegraph, telephone, elevator, and all modern conveniences. The St. James has become known as "the commercial man's friend"—capacious, excellent table, and courteous attention. The Newcomb and Ackley Houses are hotels which may be commended to the visitor to Davenport, while there are several smaller, though reliable, houses.

The Harper House, Rock Island, enjoys the well-earned reputation of being the best hotel, in all respects, in Illinois, outside of Chicago. Its business is large, its cuisine first-class, and its furnishings elegant. The Rock Island, Taylor, and Commercial Houses will prove satisfactory to sojourners content with comfort at less expense.

The Keator House, Moline, is a four-story, well-furnished, excellently managed hotel, meeting the wants of the city. Peal's Hotel does a good business, always giving satisfaction to its guests.

In connection with the Kimball House, Davenport, is the Burtis Opera House, seating 1,700 persons. It is supplied with upholstered opera chairs, large stage, and beautiful scenery, ample for the setting of any play.

The German Theater has a seating capacity of 1,000. An excellent stock company has been maintained for twenty years, and plays presented once a week or oftener. It is the oldest German theater in the West.

Harper's Theater, Rock Island, is the parlor opera house of the state. It seats 1,200, has complete and splendid scenery, opera chairs, and is attractively furnished.

Wagner's Opera House, Moline, was opened late in 1882. It is a complete theater, seating 900; has chairs, is finely frescoed, and well supplied with scenery.

CHAPTER XXX.

NOTABLE INSTITUTIONS.

Academy of Sciences.

AN institution which has carried the good name of Davenport to more places, and to more learned people the world over, than any other, is the Davenport Academy of Natural Sciences. No visitor to these cities should fail to call at this Academy, which of itself will repay a journey of many miles. Its equal is not to be found in Iowa, and, in some departments, not in the country. The collection of mound relics, for instance, is incomparable. The Academy building was erected, for the purpose which it serves, upon a beautiful lot, the gift of Mrs. P. V. Newcomb. The institution has 175 regular and 60 life members. The library is a most valuable collection, which was enlarged by more than 2,000 books, pamphlets, and papers, last year. The number of visitors in 1882 was about 6,000, of whom 1,800 were non-residents. Three volumes of proceedings — works of acknowledged scientific value — have been published.

Soldiers' Orphans' Home.

The Iowa Soldiers' Orphans' Home and Home for Indigent Children is a state charitable institution. There are 210 children at the Home, of whom 72 are soldiers' orphans. In connection with the institution are thoroughly graded schools, with competent teachers, and an industrial department for both boys and girls. Since the establishment of the Home, over 1,600 children have been cared for and educated—fitted to fight for themselves, with more than an even chance of winning success. Suitable buildings, on the cottage plan, have been provided, at a cost of $35,000, and connected with the Home are 40 acres of land. The expense of maintenance yearly is nearly $15,000. The state allowance for each child is $10, while the actual cost of support has been $8.33. S. W. Pierce is Superintendent in charge, and Mrs. Pierce, Matron.

Cook's Home for the Friendless.

This charity was made possible by the munificence of Mrs. Clarissa C. Cook, lately deceased. Her will designated the sum of $50,000 for the purpose of providing a home for "destitute and indigent females." To this sum $65,000 has been added by the closing of the estate. The will also devised for the specified object fifteen acres of land in West Davenport. Upon this, at a cost of $25,000, has been erected a building adapted, in every particular, for a home, and it is now doing its noble work. The affairs are directed by a Board of Managers.

COOK'S HOME FOR THE FRIENDLESS.

Mercy Hospital.

No institution of Davenport is pointed out with more satisfaction than Mercy Hospital, the control and discipline of which is held by the Sisters of Mercy. The grounds cover twenty acres. The main building is a massive brick of four stories, 150 by 60 feet, containing the sick wards. A building of two stories, 40 by 60 feet, is devoted to the care of the insane; and a third building, of similar size, is used for a Catholic Orphans' Asylum. The afflicted, disabled, and indigent here find tender care and medical treatment.

Young Men's Christian Association.

The Young Men's Christian Association of Davenport is now in its sixteenth year. It has quarters in pleasant rooms, which are always open to the public. It has a library, free reading-room, and frequent social and literary entertainments.

ARMORY AND ARSENAL SHOPS WHEN IN PROCESS OF ERECTION.

CHAPTER XXXI.

CHURCHES AND SOCIETIES.

"CITIES of Churches" would not be an inapt way in which to characterize this triangle of sixty thousand people, which has hundreds of thousands of dollars invested in church edifices, numbering not less than fifty-five. Several of these are fine architectural structures, and all mark the virtue and morality, no less than the intelligence and religious interests, of the people.

GRACE CATHEDRAL, DAVENPORT.

Davenport is a See city, being the seat of the Protestant Episcopal Church for the Diocese of Iowa. Rt. Rev. William Stevens Perry, Bishop. Grace Cathedral, a grand Gothic edifice, cost more than $80,000, and, with its handsome grounds, upon which is the Bishop's vine-covered residence, occupies a block. Trinity Episcopal Church has a chime of bells costing $6,000, and their peals may be heard for miles. This city is also the place of residence of the Bishop of the Roman Catholic Diocese of Davenport, embracing the southern half of the state of Iowa. Davenport has four Baptist, four Catholic, one Christian, two Congregational, four Episcopal, one Hebrew, three Lutheran, four Methodist, four Presbyterian, and one Unitarian, churches.

Rock Island, too, is not without its fine church buildings, one of which is the Broadway Presbyterian, representing a cost of $35,000. This city has two Baptist, two Catholic, two Christian, two Episcopal, two Lutheran, three Methodist, and four Presbyterian churches.

The Congregational church of Moline was erected at an outlay of not less than $40,000. The Swedish Lutheran edifice cost $25,000. There are in this city ten churches—two Baptist, one Catholic, one Congregational, two Lutheran, three Methodist, and one United Brethren.

Societies and Orders.

Of the various fraternities, orders, societies, and brotherhoods, the number is surprisingly large, and the membership numerous. Brief mention must suffice here, as the initiated member will have no difficulty in finding the hand of a brother. There are two Commanderies of Knights Templar and nine Masonic Lodges; twelve Lodges and Encampments of Odd Fellows; fourteen Lodges of Ancient Order United Workmen; six Lodges of United Brotherhood; four of Knights of Pythias; seven Groves of Druids; three Turner societies; three gun clubs; three companies of militia; three boat clubs, etc.

CHAPTER XXXII.

BUSINESS ASSOCIATIONS.

Davenport Board of Trade.

THE Davenport Board of Trade is an organization of one hundred and fifty business men, whose object is thus expressed:

"To collect and record such local and general statistical information relating to commerce and manufactures as may promote the interests of Davenport, and to protect and advance the welfare of the commercial and manufacturing, and all other classes of citizens; to promote just and equitable principles in trade; to establish uniformity in the commercial usages of the city."

A. F. Williams is President, and L. F. Parker, Secretary.

Rock Island Business Men's Association.

The Business Men's Association of Rock Island is an association of more than one hundred public-spirited citizens, who at all times act for the best interests of the city, offering encouragement to manufacturing enterprises and to strangers desirous of embarking in business here. The officers are J. W. Stewart, President, and J. F. Robinson, Secretary.

Moline.

The Moline Water Power Company, of which Charles Atkinson is President, and J. M. Gould, Secretary, holds out inducements to persons wishing to engage in manufacturing or to become residents, and offers great advantages of location.

The Moline Board of Trade has a membership comprising the public-spirited manufacturers and merchants. The officers are: Hon. J. M. Gould, President; H. A. Barnard, Vice-President; S. H. Velie, Secretary; J. W. Warr, Treasurer; and Charles Atkinson. H. H. Hill, Thomas Dunn. C. S. Ells. James Shaw, Directors. The object of the association is sufficiently stated in the name — it is to protect the rights and advance the mercantile and manufacturing interests of citizens.

In General.

The Davenport Produce Exchange occupies a room connected with the Western Union Telegraph office, and receives daily market reports from all commercial centers. The rooms are open to strangers.

Each of the cities has a flourishing Loan, Building, and Savings Association, which prospers by helping those of small means to prosper. These institutions are of admitted benefit to the citizen of ordinary means who desires to provide himself a home on the most advantageous conditions.

CHAPTER XXXIII.

BLACK HAWK'S WATCH-TOWER.

THIS historic spot, the subject of two illustrations, was the resort of the Indian chief Black Hawk. It is situated three miles south of the city of Rock Island, on the highest bank of Rock River, and was selected by the great Sac's father as a lookout at the first building of the tribe's village. From its commanding sum-

BLACK HAWK'S WATCH-TOWER, LOOKING EAST.

mit, an unobstructed view is had up and down the valley of the winding river for many miles, and across the low lands to the south. For the last half a century, the Tower has been the admiration of thousands, and now that the street-car carries the visitor to the very peak, it is the popular resort of resident and tourist. The owner, Hon. Bailey Davenport, has erected a summer-house at the most charming point of view, which is open to all.

Black Hawk, in his autobiography, which was dictated to Antoine Le Claire in 1833, and which has recently been published by Colonel J. B. Patterson. says of this interesting place: "This tower, to which my name has been applied, was a favorite resort, and was frequently visited by me alone, when I could sit and smoke my pipe, and look with wonder and pleasure at the grand scenes that were presented by the sun's rays, even across the mighty water [the Mississippi]. On one occasion, a Frenchman who had been making his home in our village brought his violin with him to the tower, to play and dance for the amusement of our people, who had assembled there. and, while dancing with his back to the cliff, accidentally fell over it and was killed by the fall. The Indians say that always, at the same time of the year. soft strains of the violin can be heard near that spot."

Another legend is related by Black Hawk. In 1827, a young Sioux Indian who was lost in a snow-storm found his way into a camp of the Sacs. While there he fell in love with a beautiful maiden, and, upon leaving for his own country, promised to return during the approaching summer and claim his bride. He did so, secreting himself in the woods until he met the object of his love. A heavy thunder-storm was coming on at the time. The lovers hastened to and took shelter under a cliff of rocks on the south side of the tower. Soon after they had done so, a loud peal of thunder was heard, the cliff of rocks was shattered into a thousand pieces, and the lovers buried beneath them. "This," writes Black Hawk, "their unexpected tomb, still remains undisturbed."

BLACK HAWK'S WATCH TOWER.

CHAPTER XXXIV.

METEOROLOGICAL SUMMARY.

BY ROBT. R. MARTIN, UNITED STATES SIGNAL OFFICER.

THE following summaries and tables are calculated from the observations taken at 6:6 A. M., 2:6 P. M., and 10:6 P. M., daily, for the period of eleven years, from 1872 to 1882 inclusive.

Atmospheric Pressure.

Table No. 1 gives the monthly and annual means of the actual barometer (corrected for temperature and instrumental error only), from which it will be seen that the atmospheric pressure is greatest in January, whence it decreases until June, thence increases gradually until January. The pressure is greatest at 6 A. M., and least at 2 P. M. The monthly range of the barometer is greatest in February, when it averages 1.187 inches, and least in August, when its average is 0.472 inch. For the seasons the average range is as follows: Spring, 0.952 inch; summer, 0.565 inch; autumn, 0.892 inch; winter, 1.115 inches. The mean annual actual barometer is 29.369 inches; reduced to sea-level, 30.037 inches.

Temperature.

Table No. 2 shows the mean temperature for each month and year, from which it will be seen that July is the warmest month, with an average temperature of 75.4°; August next, 73.9°; and January is the coldest month, with an average of 22.6°. The average annual temperature for eleven years is 49.7°. The average of the highest daily temperatures recorded is 73.8°, and the highest point reached by the thermometer on any one day was 98°, on July 5th and 6th, 1874. The average of lowest daily temperatures is 24.1°, and the lowest point reached by the thermometer on any one day, to the present date, was −23° (below zero), on January 22d, 1883, giving an extreme absolute range of temperature of 121°. The average temperature of July at 2 P. M., the hottest part of the day, is 81.9°, and the average temperature of January at 6 A. M., the coldest part of the day, is 17.9°.

For the seasons, the average temperature is as follows: Spring, 48.7°; summer, 73.3°; autumn, 51.2°; winter, 26°. The mean difference between spring and summer being 24.6°; summer and autumn, 22.1°; autumn and winter, 25.2°; and between summer and winter, a mean difference of 47.3°. The average temperature of all the warmest summer days is 82.6°, and the average of all the coldest winter days, 3.6°. The mean temperature of spring does not materially differ from that of the year. Sometimes a greater degree of cold is experienced in March than in February: thus, March, 1877, was 7.6° colder than the month that preceded it. Generally, however, the measure of heat increases gradually from month to month.

The coldest year was 1875, with an average temperature of 45.5°, and the warmest year 1878, with an average temperature of 52.2°.

Table No. 3 gives the highest and lowest temperatures and range of temperature from 1873 to 1882, inclusive.

Table No. 5 gives the dates of earliest and latest frosts and snowfalls to date.

The total number of days on which the maximum and minimum thermometers recorded temperatures below 32° can be seen by referring to Table No. 4.

Relative Humidity.

The degree of relative humidity or moisture of the atmosphere is, like the extremes and changes of temperature, of very great importance. The effects of climate upon the health depend greatly upon the humidity or dampness of the air.

Table No. 7 gives the monthly and annual averages of relative humidity, showing that the average percentage is greatest in January and least in May; and for the seasons, least in spring and greatest in winter. The means of summer and autumn do not differ materially from each other. The average annual humidity is 69.1 per cent, indicating a moderately dry climate, according to the following classification: "Moderately dry, 56 to 70; moderately moist, 71 to 85; excessively moist, 86 to 100. The most pleasant degree is 70, or thereabouts."

Rainfall.

Table No. 8 gives the total amounts of rain and melted snow, with monthly and annual averages. The table shows that the precipitation is greatest in June, when it averages 5.34 inches, and least in February, when its average is 1.37 inches. The average monthly rainfall is about 3 inches, and the average annual rainfall, 36.13 inches. The greatest amount of rain that fell on any one day was 3.73 inches, on September 18th, 1874. Most of the rainfall occurred during the night or in the eight hours ending at 6 A. M., and least in the eight hours ending at 10 P. M.

Wind.

The most prevalent wind is the NW., and the order of winds relative to frequency is as follows: NW., SW., W., E., NE., S., SE., N., the first being the most and the last the least frequent. Easterly winds are more prevalent in spring than in any other season of the year. The prevailing winds of spring and summer are SW.; of autumn and winter, NW.

Clouds.

Table No. 4 shows the average cloudiness for months and seasons (scale 0 to 10).

The most cloudy month is December, with an average of 6.1, and August the least cloudy, with an average of 4.2. The afternoon is usually the most cloudy part of the day, and the night least cloudy. During the eleven years from 1872 to 1882, the percentage of clear days was 29 per cent; fair days, 41 per cent; and cloudy days, 30 per cent.

Climate.

The climate of this locality is decidedly temperate, but it is not an equable one. In common with a large part of the Mississippi Valley, the climate is subject to comparatively great extremes; yet these extremes never reach the excessive cold of Minnesota nor the higher temperature of Missouri. Its geographical position, approximating the center of the continent, exempts it from the extreme changes which occur in the older states of the East, nearer the Atlantic coast. In its sanitary relations, the general climate is favorable, made so by a desirable combination of the means of heat and cold, rain, sunshine, and humidity. The daily changes of temperature are considerable; there is a full share of humidity, and sufficient rains. It is well adapted to the growth of all kinds of grain and other crops. The variable character of the climate is reflected in the energy and activity of the people, and is favorable to the growth of a strong, active, and hardy race.

TABLE NO. 1.—Showing Monthly and Annual Means of Actual Barometer (corrected for Temperature and Instrumental error only), from 1872 to 1882, inclusive, at Davenport, Iowa, from the Records of the U. S. Signal Office, located southwest cor. Second and Main Sts.

YEAR.	JAN.	FEB.	MARCH.	APRIL.	MAY.	JUNE.	JULY.	AUGUST.	SEPT.	OCT.	NOV.	DEC.	ANNUAL MEANS.
1872	29.445	29.354	29.416	29.273	......	29.302	29.327	29.380	29.395	29.418	29.400	29.554	*29.380
1873	29.370	29.372	29.348	29.231	29.265	29.277	29.353	29.393	29.379	29.399	29.355	29.442	29.349
1874	29.439	29.441	29.396	29.303	29.311	29.297	29.347	29.346	29.391	29.474	29.456	29.499	29.399
1875	29.504	29.468	29.333	29.357	29.282	29.318	29.334	29.340	29.408	29.347	29.413	29.273	29.370
1876	29.415	29.376	29.344	29.312	29.316	29.232	29.349	29.370	29.361	29.300	29.371	29.477	29.352
1877	29.497	29.535	29.401	29.302	29.351	29.272	29.337	29.309	29.360	29.359	29.408	29.437	29.381
1878	29.380	29.305	29.263	29.120	29.278	29.294	29.337	29.291	29.404	29.363	29.398	29.456	29.325
1879	29.485	29.441	29.428	29.346	29.338	29.325	29.313	29.326	29.442	29.450	29.404	29.421	29.314
1880	29.338	29.358	29.401	29.271	29.307	29.294	29.334	29.353	29.395	29.386	29.531	29.462	29.370
1881	29.478	29.431	29.254	29.364	29.349	29.271	29.374	29.354	29.274	29.407	29.409	29.441	29.357
1882	29.463	29.352	29.374	29.343	29.317	29.246	29.375	29.354	29.428	29.328	29.468	29.431	29.373
Means of 11 years	29.447	29.403	29.360	29.289	†29.311	29.284	29.344	29.348	29.377	29.386	29.419	29.445	29.369

* Mean for 11 months. † Mean of ten years.

TABLE NO. 2.—Showing the Mean Temperature for each month and year, from 1872 to 1882, inclusive, at Davenport, Iowa, from the Records of the U. S. Signal Office, located at the southwest corner of Second and Main Streets.

YEAR.	JAN.	FEB.	MARCH.	APRIL.	MAY.	JUNE.	JULY.	AUGUST.	SEPT.	OCT.	NOV.	DEC.	ANNUAL MEANS.
1872	22.6	27.1	32.3	51.2	61.7	72.5	75.5	74.2	64.8	51.6	32.4	18.2	48.7
1873	17.1	23.4	36.5	46.3	59.1	77.7	75.2	78.1	62.3	48.3	33.5	29.6	49.0
1874	23.7	25.9	34.3	41.2	64.3	72.6	77.5	74.3	65.1	52.3	36.3	27.9	49.6
1875	9.4	10.4	30.1	45.7	60.5	68.4	73.6	69.3	61.7	48.6	33.4	34.5	45.5
1876	29.9	30.1	32.1	50.6	62.1	69.0	75.4	74.6	62.5	49.2	35.2	15.4	48.8
1877	16.8	36.3	28.7	49.4	61.6	69.1	75.0	72.5	67.1	53.5	37.1	42.5	50.8
1878	30.1	36.7	48.2	54.7	57.5	68.0	78.0	74.0	65.1	51.8	42.3	20.3	52.2
1879	18.4	25.5	39.5	50.5	53.8	69.5	76.9	71.7	60.5	59.8	38.9	23.8	49.2
1880	37.6	32.9	37.0	49.7	67.2	72.2	74.5	74.5	62.8	50.7	30.7	21.8	51.0
1881	13.8	19.9	28.8	44.6	69.0	69.7	77.6	77.2	69.8	56.5	39.7	38.2	50.4
1882	28.9	40.3	40.3	51.3	55.6	68.6	70.5	72.2	64.4	57.7	42.2	28.2	51.7
Means of 11 years	22.6	28.0	35.3	48.7	61.1	70.7	75.4	73.9	64.2	52.7	36.6	27.3	49.7

Examined and corrected at the office of the Chief Signal Officer, U. S. Army, Washington, D. C., on May 29th and 31st, 1883.

ROBT. R. MARTIN,
Sergt. Signal Corps, U. S. A.

TABLE NO. 3.—Showing Maximum, Minimum, and Range of Temperature for each U. S. Signal Office, at the southwest

YEAR.	JAN.			FEB.			MARCH.			APRIL.			MAY.			JUNE.		
	Highest.	Lowest.	Range.	Highest.	Lowest.	Range.	Highest.	Lowest.	Range.	Highest.	Lowest.	Range.	Highest.	Lowest.	Range.	Highest.	Lowest.	Range.
1873	44	-20	64	45	-10	55	57	-6	63	80	31	49	83	40	43	92	56	36
1874	60	-10	70	48	-4	52	61	13	48	73	21	52	90	41	49	93	52	41
1875	39	-22	61	39	-16	55	74	1	73	75	18	57	87	29	58	90	45	45
1876	58	0	58	62	-5	67	70	7	63	72	30	42	87	33	54	88	43	45
1877	53	-11	64	59	18	41	66	0	66	73	22	51	85	35	50	86	44	42
1878	49	0	49	58	17	41	73	29	44	76	35	41	81	36	45	88	48	40
1879	50	-19	69	50	-3	53	71	8	63	81	20	61	86	33	53	88	48	40
1880	56	17	39	62	7	55	64	8	56	79	29	50	89	45	44	89	51	38
1881	40	-21	61	48	-7	55	45	7	38	77	16	61	88	38	50	89	51	38
1882	58.2	0	58.2	66.7	6	60.7	64.7	10	54.7	78.2	28	50.2	78.7	33	45.7	89.2	43	46.2

TABLE NO. 4.—Showing the Means and Extremes of Pressure, Temperature, Rainfall, U. S. Signal Office, at the southwest

SEASON.	MONTH.	ACTUAL BAROMETER. Corrected for Temperature and Instrumental Error.			
		Mean.	Highest.	Lowest.	Range.
SPRING.	March	29.360	30.021	28.350	1.671
	April	29.299	29.859	28.574	1.285
	May	29.311	29.846	28.671	1.175
	Average	29.323	Highest, 30.021	Lowest, 28.350	Absolute Range, 1.671
SUMMER.	June	29.284	29.715	28.616	1.099
	July	29.343	29.669	28.938	0.731
	August	29.348	29.710	29.026	0.684
	Average	29.325	Highest, 29.715	Lowest, 28.616	Absolute Range, 1.099
AUTUMN.	September	29.378	29.784	28.872	0.912
	October	29.386	29.953	28.653	1.300
	November	29.419	29.998	28.480	1.518
	Average	29.394	Highest, 29.998	Lowest, 28.480	Absolute Range, 1.518
WINTER.	December	29.445	30.120	28.571	1.549
	January	29.417	30.085	28.564	1.521
	February	29.403	30.066	28.484	1.582
	Average	29.432	Highest, 30.120	Lowest, 28.484	Absolute Range, 1.636

NOTE.—The sign minus (-) denotes below zero.

Examined and corrected at the office of the Chief Signal Officer, U. S. Army, Washington, D. C., on May 29th and 31st, 1883.

Month and Year. at Davenport, Iowa, from 1873 to 1882, inclusive, from the Records of the corner of Second and Main Streets.

	July.			August.			Sept.			Oct.			Nov.			Dec.			Year.		
	Highest.	Lowest.	Range.	Highest.	Lowest.	Range.	Highest.	Lowest.	Range.	Highest.	Lowest.	Range.	Highest.	Lowest.	Range.	Highest.	Lowest.	Range.	Highest.	Lowest.	Range.
	o	o	o	o	o	o	o	o	o	o	o	o	o	o	o	o	o	o	o	o	o
	93	61	32	85	60	25	86	37	49	74	18	56	62	7	55	59	7	52	95	-20	115
	98	56	42	95	58	37	89	43	46	77	29	48	71	0	71	54	-8	62	98	-10	108
	92	58	34	86	48	28	88	37	51	73	29	44	56	-3	54	50	-6	56	92	-22	114
	90	57	33	90	53	37	79	41	38	75	25	50	65	8	57	47	-17	64	90	-17	107
	92	55	37	88	53	35	86	47	39	82	34	48	57	7	50	63	20	43	92	-11	103
	95	56	39	90	56	34	86	41	45	80	23	57	59	25	34	46	-7	53	95	-7	102
	94	58	36	90	50	40	81	36	45	85	24	61	71	15	56	57	-14	71	94	-19	113
	94	52	42	93	52	41	86	43	43	78	24	54	64	1	63	52	-14	66	94	-14	108
	94	57	37	96.3	53.5	42.8	94	46	48	79	37	42	60	6	59	55	12	43	96.3	-21	117.3
M.	93.7	53	35.7	88.7		52	26.7	88.7	43	45.7	79.7	36	43.7	68.7		19	49.7	49.7	-15	64.7	89.2	-15	104.2

Clouds, Winds, etc., from 1872 to 1882, inclusive, at Davenport, Iowa, from the Records of the corner of Second and Main Streets.

	Thermometer.					Number of Days.			Mean Relative Humidity.	Rainfall. Inch. & Hundth.		Av'rag. Cloudiness. (Scale, 0 to 10.)	Prevailing Direction of Wind.
Mean.	Highest.	Lowest.	Range.	Warmest Day.	Coldest Day.	Maximum below 32°.	Minimum below 32°.	Maximum above 90°.		Mean.	Greatest Daily Am't.		
o	o	o	o	o	o	*	*						
35.3	74	-6	80	63.3	8.0	53	214	0	70.3	2.42	1.61	5.6	NW
48.7	81	16	65	70.3	20.7	3	54	0	62.7	3.26	3.04	5.3	NE & NW
61.1	90	29	61	80.7	37.0	0	0	0	62.6	4.43	2.79	4.9	E
	Hi'-est,	Lo'-est,	Abso. Rng.	Warm-est,	Cold-est,	Total No. Days.					Great-est,		
48.4	90	-6	96	80.7	8.0	56	268	0	65.2	10.11	3.04	5.3	NW
70.7	93	43	50	86.3	48.3	0	0	10	69.7	5.34	3.50	5.2	SW
75.4	98	52	46	87.7	60.3	0	0	41	68.3	4.05	3.11	4.4	SW
73.9	96.3	48	48.3	87.3	59.0	0	0	29	68.1	3.70	2.70	4.2	SW
	Hi'-est,	Lo'-est,	Abso. Rng.	Warm-est,	Cold-est,	Total No. Days.					Great-est,		
73.3	98	43	55	87.7	48.3	0	0	80	68.7	13.09	3.50	4.6	SW
64.2	94	36	58	84.7	44.0	0	0	3	68.9	3.66	3.73	4.5	SW
52.7	85	18	67	77.0	25.0	0	24	0	66.6	2.56	2.29	5.0	SW
36.6	71	-3	74	64.3	2.0	45	163	0	69.8	1.92	1.49	5.9	NW
	Hi'-est,	Lo'-est,	Abso. Rng.	Warm-est,	Cold-est,	Total No. Days.					Great-est,		
51.2	94	-3	97	84.7	2.0	45	187	3	68.4	8.14	3.73	5.1	SW
27.3	63	-17	80	59.0	-9.0	128	256	0	73.8	1.58	1.39	6.1	NW
22.6	60	-22	82	51.3	-16.3	179	299	0	75.4	1.80	1.85	5.6	W
28.1	66.7	-16	82.7	53.0	-6.7	108	246	0	72.9	1.37	2.07	5.4	NW
	Hi'-est,	Lo'-est,	Abso. Rng.	Warm-est,	Cold-est,	Total No. Days.					Great-est,		
26.0	66.7	-22	88.7	59.0	-16.3	415	801	0	74.0	4.75	2.07	5.7	NW

*January, February, March, and April, from 1873 to 1883, inclusive.
May to December, 1872 to 1882, inclusive.

Robt. R. Martin,
Sergt. Signal Corps, U. S. A.

TABLE NO. 5.—Showing date of Earliest and Latest Frosts and Snowfalls, at Davenport, Iowa, from 1872, from the Records of the U. S. Signal Office, southwest corner of Second and Main Streets.

WINTER OF.	FROST.		SNOW.	
	Date of Earliest.	Date of Latest.	Date of Earliest.	Date of Latest.
1871 – 1872	Station opened, May 24, 1871.			April 15, 1872
1872 – 1873	Oct. 23, 1872	April 29, 1873	Nov. 14, 1872	April 24, 1873
1873 – 1874	Sept. 19, 1873	April 29, 1874	Oct. 22, 1873	April 27, 1874
1874 – 1875	Oct. 12, 1874	May 6, 1875	Oct. 30, 1874	April 16, 1875
1875 – 1876	Sept. 18, 1875	May 23, 1876	Oct. 26, 1875	Mar. 28, 1876
1876 – 1877	Sept. 27, 1876	May 2, 1877	Nov. 6, 1876	April 29, 1877
1877 – 1878	Sept. 18, 1877	May 13, 1878	Nov. 1, 1877	Mar. 30, 1878
1878 – 1879	Sept. 11, 1878	April 18, 1879	Oct. 26, 1878	April 2, 1879
1879 – 1880	Sept. 19, 1879	April 30, 1880	Nov. 1, 1879	Mar. 18, 1880
1880 – 1881	Oct. 4, 1880	May 3, 1881	Oct. 16, 1880	April 12, 1881
1881 – 1882	Oct. 5, 1881	May 24, 1882	Nov. 11, 1881	May 23, 1882
1882 – 1883	Oct. 17, 1882	May 22, 1883	Nov. 25, 1882	April 6, 1883

TABLE NO. 6.—Showing the Highest and Lowest Stages of Water, with Dates of same, of the Mississippi River, at Davenport, Iowa, on the gauge now in use on the draw-pier of the Government Bridge, from 1860 to 1882, inclusive.

YEAR.	HIGH WATER. Ft. and Tenths.	DATE.	LOW WATER. Ft. and Tenths.	DATE.
1860	12 ft. .3	March 3	1 ft. .7	Sept. 4 to 7
1861	13.7	March 2	1.5	Dec. 8 and 9
1862	16.55	May 5 to 8	0.95	December 12
1863	9.3	May 1 to 4	1.25	Aug. 9 and 10
1864	8.9	February 27	0.34	November 29
1865	11.7	April 23 and 24	1.90	December 12
1866	16.45	May 4	2.40	Oct. 23 and 24
1867	15.15	June 28 and 29	1.65	Dec. 7 and 8
1868	15.2	March 11	1.6	December 16
1869	13.2	Oct. 9 and 10	2.4	March 25
1870	17.0	April 24 and 25	2.2	December 21
1871	13.2	May 14 to 16	1.0	November 27
1872	9.4	May 28	0.65	November 24
1873	14.2	March 15	0.75	December 1
1874	15.75	March 10	0.4	December 3
1875	12.95	April 29	0.1	November 27
1876	13.35	April 17	1.4	January 12
1877	9.95	April 4	0.75	September 25
1878	7.15	July 17	Zero.	Dec. 14 and 15
1879	7.85	June 1	1.05	October 1
1880	18.4	June 26	1.2	February 2
1881	17.7	Oct. 25 to 27	2.6	August 26
1882	14.1	April 23	1.7	January 8

ROBT. R. MARTIN,
Sergt. Signal Corps, U. S. A.

TABLE NO. 7.—Showing Mean Percentage of Relative Humidity of the Atmosphere for each month and year, from 1872 to 1882, inclusive, at Davenport, Iowa, from the Records of the U. S. Signal Office, located southwest corner Second and Main Streets.

Year.	Jan.	Feb.	March.	April.	May.	June.	July.	August.	Sept.	Oct.	Nov.	Dec.	Annual Means.
1872	76.4	73.1	68.3	60.7	....	67.8	70.4	75.4	69.8	60.5	68.7	71.9	*69.4
1873	76.2	69.7	62.4	68.8	69.1	63.6	64.6	56.0	61.6	63.9	71.7	81.1	67.4
1874	82.6	83.2	77.2	65.2	58.3	68.5	64.1	66.9	74.9	72.4	74.4	81.4	72.4
1875	83.0	87.4	78.9	60.6	62.2	72.1	73.3	69.7	70.0	62.9	68.5	76.8	72.1
1876	76.3	71.4	74.4	59.9	64.0	71.7	70.3	63.3	72.5	60.4	73.5	75.4	69.9
1877	78.0	68.3	73.4	60.2	60.2	69.6	65.8	67.5	67.0	75.1	75.0	77.7	69.8
1878	75.9	73.2	67.5	63.6	68.9	68.6	69.2	72.5	68.9	64.3	69.6	75.2	69.8
1879	70.1	69.4	69.1	56.7	57.9	68.6	66.6	68.6	67.1	64.3	67.3	71.1	66.4
1880	74.9	66.9	63.4	61.4	58.3	70.1	70.0	69.0	68.9	63.7	63.7	71.5	66.8
1881	73.0	77.6	75.2	69.4	53.6	70.9	66.5	59.4	64.9	73.7	66.5	65.0	68.5
1882	62.9	61.3	63.6	63.5	67.1	74.9	70.3	74.3	72.5	72.0	63.3	64.8	68.0
Means of 11 years	75.4	72.9	70.3	62.7	†62.6	69.7	68.3	68.1	68.9	66.6	69.8	73.8	69.1

* Mean of 11 months.   † Mean of ten years.

TABLE NO. 8.—Showing amounts of Rain and Melted Snow for each month and year, from 1872 to 1882, inclusive, at Davenport, Iowa, from the Records of the U. S. Signal Office, located at the southwest corner of Second and Main Streets.

Year.	Jan.	Feb.	March.	April.	May.	June.	July.	August.	Sept.	Oct.	Nov.	Dec.	Total for Year.
1872	0.13	0.10	1.82	5.06	4.46	3.78	3.80	8.91	5.30	0.61	1.86	0.61	36.44
1873	3.56	0.77	1.43	3.96	6.37	2.16	2.37	0.51	1.00	1.48	0.63	3.84	28.08
1874	4.34	0.74	1.34	2.64	3.45	5.37	3.10	3.68	7.86	1.30	2.47	0.50	36.79
1875	0.38	1.09	0.88	2.30	2.01	4.91	9.36	1.73	4.05	1.63	0.57	3.08	31.99
1876	3.47	3.63	4.35	5.39	6.70	4.25	4.82	4.27	5.50	1.54	2.54	0.36	46.82
1877	1.41	0.07	3.91	3.28	2.82	5.80	3.42	3.21	1.45	4.88	2.53	2.32	35.10
1878	0.36	1.09	2.21	2.89	5.14	4.36	2.19	5.07	1.82	4.21	0.90	0.97	31.21
1879	0.79	1.09	1.80	1.54	5.83	4.57	5.87	4.33	1.43	0.92	4.70	1.02	33.89
1880	3.13	1.72	2.68	4.50	5.09	7.21	4.31	5.90	4.87	0.94	1.23	1.15	42.73
1881	1.34	4.14	3.33	1.11	1.34	7.94	0.91	0.83	5.59	6.85	2.19	1.71	37.28
1882	0.90	0.62	2.90	3.15	5.49	8.43	4.41	2.29	1.39	3.75	1.47	1.78	36.60
Means of 11 years	1.80	1.37	2.42	3.26	4.43	5.34	4.05	3.70	3.66	2.56	1.92	1.58	36.08

Examined and corrected at the office of the Chief Signal Officer, U. S. Army,
  Washington, D. C., on May 29th and 31st, 1883.

ROBT. R. MARTIN,
Sergt. Signal Corps, U. S. A.

JAMES J. PARKS. ADAIR PLEASANTS. **PARKS & PLEASANTS,** **Attorneys at Law** Rooms 1 and 2 Buford's Block, ROCK ISLAND, ILL.	**FRED. G. CLAUSEN,** **ARCHITECT.** *Office In Der Demokrat Building,* *Second Floor,* West Third St. DAVENPORT, IOWA.
W. S. CAMERON & SON, The Edison Light **HATTERS** A FULL LINE OF →Men's Furnishing Goods← And Hats, ready at all times for inspection. *⁎*⁎* New supplies being received daily. 127 East Third St. Davenport, Iowa.	N. C. MARTIN, Sec. E. S. CARL, Treas. **Davenport Oat Meal Co.** STEEL CUT A. B. & C. **OAT MEAL.** Mills, Cor. Fifth and Iowa Streets, **Davenport, Iowa.** *Board of Directors.*—J. H. Murphy, President; J. F. O'Connor, Vice-President; F. H. Miller, F. H. Griggs, C. F. Knappe.

MORGAN & McCANDLESS,

DENTAL ROOMS,

Library Building,   DAVENPORT, IOWA.

THE MOST COMPLETE AND FINEST OFFICE IN THE STATE.

Continuous Gum Plate Work and Gold Fillings with the Electric Mallet made only at this office. We do a greater variety of work than any other office in the State, and guarantee the best satisfaction or refund the money. Nitrous Oxide Gas
J. B. MORGAN, D.D.S. | administered for the painless extraction of teeth. | A. W. M'CANDLESS, D.D.S.

PIONEER AND LARGEST

Furniture and   ✳

✳   **Carpet House**

→ROCK·ISLAND,·ILL.←

H. A. BARNARD, President.   J. SILAS LEAS, Vice-Pres.   W. C. BENNETT, Sec and Treas.

BARNARD & LEAS MFG. CO.

MANUFACTURERS OF

Victor Smutters,   Victor Brush Scourer,
Advance Brush and Smut Machine,   Barnard's Dustless Wheat Separator,
Duplex Separator and Grader,
Eureka Flour Packers,   Eureka Bran Packers,   Middlings Purifier,
Victor Corn Shellers and Dustless Corn Cleaner.

MOLINE, - - ILLINOIS.

EBI & NEUMAN,
FOUNDERS & MACHINISTS

MANUFACTURERS OF AND DEALERS IN

FARM MACHINERY,

Corner Front and Gaines Streets,   DAVENPORT, IOWA.

PHŒNIX
MILL CO.
MANUFACTURERS OF

Spring and Winter Wheat
Patent and Fancy
FAMILY
Flour

THIS MILL IS

Furnished with the Latest and Most Improved Roller System.

F. H. GRIGGS, President.
F. T. BLUNCK, Sec. and Treas.
H. POLL, Superintendent.

DAVENPORT, IOWA.

80   Three Cities and Rock Island Arsenal — Advertisements.

CASH HOUSE.   **WHOLESALE AND RETAIL.**

J. H. C. PETERSEN & SONS,
WHOLESALE AND RETAIL DEALERS IN

Dry Goods, Notions, Millinery

Carpets, Boots and Shoes, Hats and Caps, Furs, Gloves, Clothing,
Bed Feathers, and Gents' Furnishing Goods,

217, 217½, 219, and 221 West Second Street,   DAVENPORT, IOWA.
Cor. Second and State Sts., Geneseo, Ill.   234 and 236 Fifth Ave., Clinton, Iowa.

ESTABLISHED 1864.

BRYANT & DOE,
WHOLESALE
BOOTS AND SHOES

Orders Filled at Eastern Prices.

207 and 209 Brady Street,   DAVENPORT, IOWA.

ESTABLISHED 1857.

JENS LORENZEN,
IMPORTER OF AND DEALER IN

China, Crockery and Glassware,

223 West Third St.   DAVENPORT, IOWA.

DAVENPORT WOOLEN MILLS COMPANY

FLANNELS,

→ Blankets, Yarns, and Hosiery ←

DAVENPORT, IOWA.

Correspondence Invited.

WM. RENWICK, Pres.   S. A. JENNINGS, Manager.   J. B. PHELPS, Sec. and Treas.

ESTABLISHED 1868.

MASON'S CARRIAGE WORKS,

(FORMERLY MASON & EVANS.)

119 AND 121 E. FOURTH ST.   DAVENPORT, IOWA.

FINE CARRIAGES AND HARNESS

REPOSITORY UNDER KIMBALL HOUSE.

⋘SEND FOR CATALOGUE AND PRICES.⋙

FINE ORDERED WORK A SPECIALTY.

RICHARDSON BROS.

⋖ THOROUGHBRED ⋗

JERSEY CATTLE

LARGEST HERD IN THE WEST.   SEND FOR CATALOGUE.

DAVENPORT, IOWA.

ESTABLISHED 1869.

SIEG & WILLIAMS,

DEALERS IN

Iron, Carriage Hardware,

WAGON STOCK,

Blacksmiths' Furnishing and Hard Wood Lumber,

Cor. Main and Third Streets,   DAVENPORT, IOWA.

M. D. HUGGINS,
GENERAL COMMISSION,
AND WHOLESALE DEALER IN
Fruits, Nuts, Paper Bags, Wrapping Papers, Twines, Etc.

DAVENPORT, IOWA.

MOLINE STOVE CO.
MANUFACTURERS OF
❋Cook ✦ Stoves❋

AND LIGHT GRAY IRON CASTINGS. SEND FOR PRICE LIST.

≪MOLINE, · ILLINOIS.≫

ESTABLISHED 1854.
OTTO ALBRECHT & CO.
MANUFACTURERS OF
FINE CIGARS
AND DEALERS IN ALL KINDS OF
TOBACCOS AND PIPES.
Special Brands, "Rob Roy" and "Modoc."

306 West Second Street,   DAVENPORT, IOWA.

M. M. BRIGGS,
Livery, Sale, and Feed Stable,
Cor. Nineteenth St. and Second Ave.

ROCK ISLAND, ILL.

J. M. CHRISTY,
MANUFACTURER OF
Crackers and Biscuits,
ROCK ISLAND, ILL. AND DES MOINES, IOWA.

———— SPECIALTIES : ————

THE CHRISTY OYSTER — AND CHRISTY WAFERS.

E. W. SPENCER,
DEALER IN
Stoves, Ranges, Furnaces,

Marble, Slate, Iron, and Wood Mantels, Grates of all kinds, Tile of every description, Brass Goods, Registers, Pumps, and all kinds of House-Furnishing Goods.

The best of workmen employed in the manufacture of Cornices, Creamers, Tin, Sheet-Iron, and Copper Work of all kinds, Tin and Sheet-Iron Roofing, etc.

———— ESTIMATES SENT BY MAIL. ————

1728 Second Avenue, ROCK ISLAND, ILLINOIS.

WEST DAVENPORT FURNITURE CO.
MANUFACTURERS OF ALL KINDS OF

—FURNITURE—

Illustrated Catalogue and Price List sent on application.

OFFICE, NO. 518 WARREN STREET,

DAVENPORT, IOWA.

--- THE LEADING BOOK AND STATIONERY HOUSE. ---

THOMPSON & CARMICHAEL,
Miscellaneous & School Books
BLANK BOOKS AND STATIONERY.

Finest line of Engravings, Pictures, Mouldings, and Frames in the city. *₀* Paper-Hangings and Decorations, from the Cheapest to the Finest Grades.

Cor. Brady and Third Streets,   **DAVENPORT, IOWA.**

HUGH WARNOCK.   ESTABLISHED 1853.   ROBERT RALSTON.

WARNOCK & RALSTON,
MANUFACTURERS OF
—SOAPS—
CANDLES AND LARD OIL,

Cor. Fifth Ave. and Second St.   **ROCK ISLAND, ILL.**

CHAS. BEIDERBECKE.   F. H. MILLER.

BEIDERBECKE & MILLER,
WHOLESALE GROCERS
DAVENPORT, IOWA.

D. DONALDSON,
MANUFACTURER OF

Butchers' Tools,   # SAWS   **Ice Plows, Etc.**

SAW MILL SAWS A SPECIALTY.
Cor. Fourth Ave. and Sixteenth St.   **ROCK ISLAND, ILL.**

ESTABLISHED 1857.   CORRESPONDENCE SOLICITED.

| LYMAN A. ELLIS. | J. H. MURPHY. | GEORGE E. GOULD. |

Ellis, Murphy & Gould,

⇢ Attorneys, ⇠

OFFICE:
METROPOLITAN BLOCK.

DAVENPORT, IOWA.

——) Practice in Federal and State Courts. (——

THE OLD RELIABLE
Diamond Jo Steamboat Line.

Three Boats per Week, Each Way, Between St. Louis and St. Paul.

The Steamer "Josephine" runs between Rock Island and Dubuque, connecting at Fulton and Rock Island with the leading railroads for business to or from the East, South, or West.

Mark and consign shipments care Diamond Jo Line Steamers.

JO REYNOLDS,	E. M. DICKEY,	JAMES OSBORN,	GEORGE LAMONT,
General Manager.	*Gen. Freight Agent.*	*Agent, Davenport.*	*Agent, Rock Island.*

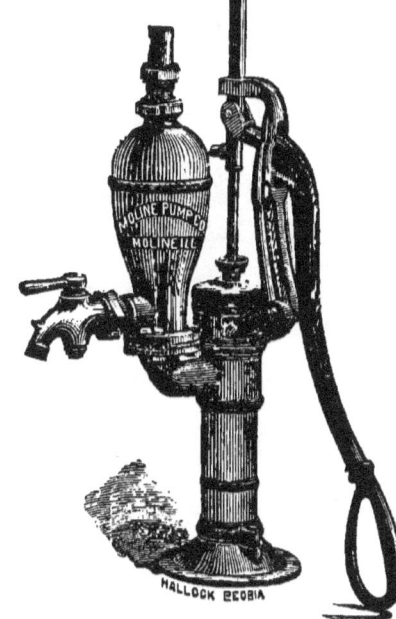

ESTABLISHED 1863. — INCORPORATED 1873.

MOLINE

MANUFACTURERS OF

IRON LIFT, FORCE AND CISTERN
PUMPS,

For Hand and Windmill Use,
and

WOOD SUCTION & CHAIN
PUMPS,

Rubber Buckets, Iron Sinks, Etc.

Also Jobbers in Iron and Lead Pipe, Malleable Fittings, Hose and Brass Goods, as well as Complete Stocks of Tools for Pump Purposes.

MOLINE, ILLINOIS.

E. W. HURST,
Fire✦and✦Life✦Insurance,

OFFICE—ROOMS 3 AND 4, MASONIC TEMPLE,
ROCK ISLAND, ILL.

H. H. FELCH, Manager.   R. F. HULL, Traveling Agent.

DAVENPORT LADDER CO.
MANUFACTURERS OF

✻Firemen's, Farmer's, Trestle, Step, and Extension Ladders.✻

The only exclusive Ladder House in the West. Lightest, cheapest, and strongest Ladder made. Also Butter-Trays, Washboards, Clothes-Racks, etc.

Office and Warerooms, Northeast Corner Fourth and LeClaire Sts., Davenport, Iowa.

St. Louis & St. Paul Packet Company

GREAT THROUGH PASSENGER ROUTE

TO ALL POINTS IN THE NORTHWEST,
ST. PAUL, MINNEAPOLIS, DULUTH, AND BISMARCK,
— AND —
ALL POINTS IN THE SOUTH AND SOUTHWEST,
ARKANSAS AND TEXAS.

The Most Direct and Cheapest Route, offering greater inducements and better accommodations, giving passengers an opportunity of visiting St. Louis, the great metropolis of the West, on their way to Arkansas, Texas, and Florida, and saving excursionists from the South a tiresome all-rail ride to the summer resorts of the great Northwest.

THROUGH TICKETS For Sale at all Principal Points, East, West, North, and South.

Further information given on application to or writing

LON BRYSON, *Agent, Davenport, Iowa.*   A. M. HUTCHINSON, *Supt., Keokuk, Iowa.*
F. L. JOHNSON, *Sec'y, St. Louis, Mo.*   W. F. DAVIDSON, *Pres., St. Paul, Minn.*

Rock Island & Peoria Railway

CENTRAL SHORT LINE.

CONNECTING LINK BETWEEN THE SOUTHEAST AND THE GREAT WEST AND NORTHWEST.

FOUR FAST PASSENGER TRAINS DAILY (EXCEPT SUNDAY),

Making close connections for all principal cities in the East, South, West, and North by most desirable routes.

Through Tickets sold at lowest rates and Baggage checked through to the smallest hamlet, as well as to the large cities.

Special attention given to the shipment of freight consigned to the care of the Rock Island & Peoria Railway at Rock Island or Peoria.

R. R. CABLE, Gen. Supt.   H. B. SUDLOW, Asst. Supt.   A. N. MORTON, Gen. Frt. and Tkt. Agt.

"BURLINGTON ROUTE"
(Chicago, Burlington & Quincy Railroad.)

GOING EAST AND WEST. Elegant Day Coaches, Parlor Cars, with Reclining Chairs (seats free), Smoking Cars, with Revolving Chairs, Pullman Palace Sleeping Cars and the famous C. B. & Q. Dining Cars run daily to and from Chicago & Kansas City, Chicago & Council Bluffs, Chicago & Des Moines, Chicago, St. Joseph, Atchison & Topeka. Only through line between Chicago, Lincoln & Denver. Through cars between Indianapolis & Council Bluffs via Peoria. All connections made in Union Depots. It is known as the great THROUGH CAR LINE.

GOING NORTH AND SOUTH. Solid Trains of Elegant Day Coaches and Pullman Palace Sleeping Cars are run daily, to and from St. Louis, via Hannibal, Quincy, Keokuk, Burlington, Cedar Rapids and Albert Lea to St. Paul and Minneapolis; Parlor Cars with Reclining Chairs to and from St. Louis and Peoria and to and from St. Louis and Ottumwa. Only one change of cars between St. Louis and Des Moines, Iowa, Lincoln, Nebraska, and Denver, Colorado.

It is universally admitted to be the **Finest Equipped Railroad in the World for all Classes of Travel.**

PERCEVAL LOWELL, Gen. Pass. Ag't, Chicago.
T. J. POTTER, 3d Vice-Pres't and Gen'l Manager

HENRY DART'S SONS,
WHOLESALE GROCERS,
ROCK ISLAND, ILL.

ESTABLISHED 1857. CORRESPONDENCE SOLICITED.

H. F. MOELLER,
MANUFACTURER OF ALL KINDS OF
WOODEN BOXES
AND THE

Patent Double-Cylinder and Greenwood Washing Machines,

DAVENPORT, IOWA.

GEO. H. YOUNG.　　　　　　　　　　　E. S. BALLORD.

GEO. H. YOUNG & CO.
WHOLESALE MANUFACTURERS.

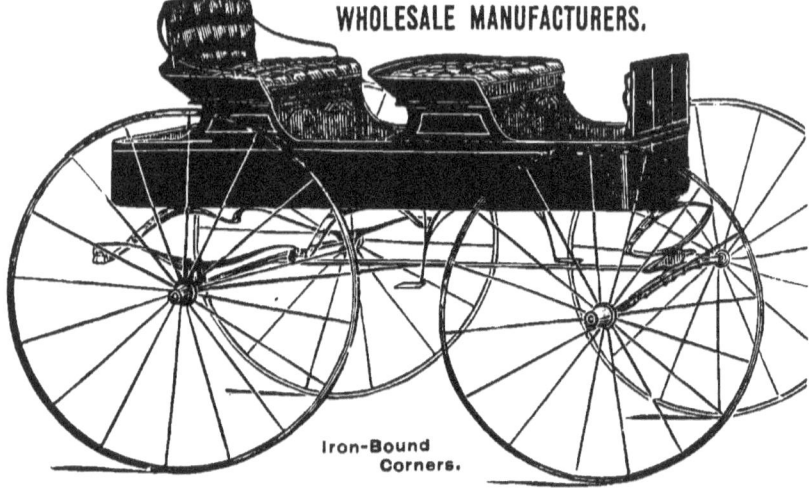

Iron-Bound Corners.

200, 202, 204, 206 East Front St.　　　**DAVENPORT, IOWA.**

REIMERS & FERNALD,
MANUFACTURING CONFECTIONERS,

—— JOBBERS IN ——

Nuts, Dates, Figs, Crackers, Cigars, Fireworks, Cove Oysters, Sardines,

PAPER BAGS, ETC.

✯DAVENPORT, IOWA.✯

Le Claire Foundry & Machine Shops,

M. DONAHUE, Proprietor.   DAVENPORT, IOWA.

MANUFACTURER OF

STEAM ENGINES,

Sugar and Corn Mills, Mill Gearing; House Work, including Columns, Window Caps and Sills, Door-Plates, etc.; Boiler Fronts, Iron Fencing and Cresting, etc.

Especial attention given to all kinds of Engine Work, Mill and Mining Machinery, and General Jobbing. Employing the best machinery and skilled workmen, full satisfaction in work is guaranteed, with the lowest prices.

"The Donahue Variable Cut-Off Engine" and the "The Donahue Excelsior Corn and Cob Mill" are specialties of our manufacture.

Orders solicited, and price lists furnished on request.

—— ESTABLISHED 1854. ——

NICHOLAS KUHNEN,

MANUFACTURER OF

✦ FINE ✦ CIGARS ✦

AND DEALER IN ALL KINDS OF

FINE-CUT, PLUG, AND SMOKING TOBACCOS,

Importer and Dealer in Leaf Tobacco.   **DAVENPORT, IOWA.**

Moline Scale Co.   -   Moline, Ill.

Manufacturers of the
Celebrated Victor
Standard

SCALES.

Hay, Stock,
Railroad, Warehouse, Dormant and
Portable Scales.

For DURABILITY,
ACCURACY,
and RELIABILITY

THE
VICTOR
HAS
NO EQUAL.

HARTZ & BAHNSEN,
WHOLESALE DRUGGISTS,

Dealers in Surgical Instruments and Physicians' Supplies,

CORRESPONDENCE SOLICITED. **ROCK ISLAND, ILL.**

T. J. ROBINSON, Pres.   J. H. WILSON, Vice-Pres.   J. F. ROBINSON, Cashier.

ROCK ISLAND NATIONAL BANK,
ROCK ISLAND, ILLINOIS.

CAPITAL STOCK, . . $100,000. | **SURPLUS FUND,** . . $50,000.
UNDIVIDED PROFITS, . $35,000.

New York Correspondent — National Park Bank.   Chicago Correspondents — Commercial National Bank and Merchants Loan and Trust Company.

ESTABLISHED 1856.

MITCHELL & LYNDE,
✳ BANKERS, ✳

P. L. MITCHELL.
CORNELIUS LYNDE.   ROCK ISLAND, ILLINOIS.
PHIL. MITCHELL.

BAILEY DAVENPORT, Pres.   JOS. ROSENFIELD, Vice-Pres.   JOHN PEETZ, Cashier.

PEOPLES NATIONAL BANK
ROCK ISLAND, ILLINOIS.

Capital, - $100,000. | **Surplus,** - $25,000.

A GENERAL BANKING BUSINESS TRANSACTED.

New York Correspondent — Importers and Traders National Bank.   Chicago Correspondent — Northwestern National Bank.

— COLLECTIONS PROMPTLY ATTENDED TO.—

J. W. STEWART. J. M. MONTGOMERY.

STEWART & MONTGOMERY,
JOBBERS OF
Hardware, Iron, Nails,

Glass, Cutlery, Cordage, Belting, Mechanics' Tools, Wagon Stock, Etc.

Agents for the Glidden Steel Barbed Fence Wire.   ROCK ISLAND, ILLINOIS.

Thos. McCullough & Son,
→Tailors←

W. J. McCULLOUGH.

318 BRADY ST.   **DAVENPORT, IOWA.**

Harper House,
BEN HARPER, Proprietor,
ROCK ISLAND, ILL.

This is one of the finest and best kept hotels in the United States. There is no other hotel in the world that is safer against fire or means of escape from fire. Watchmen patrol the halls at all hours of night. Every room has a mercury alarm, which at 110 degrees of heat alarms the office. Every floor has permanent standpipes, with direct pressure, connected with the water mains of the Holly Water Works, and hose reaching every room on each floor. The outside, from ridge to lower story, is supplied on all sides with Benner's iron balconies and permanent and safely anchored iron fire-escape ladders, perfectly safe for women or children, and can be reached from the rooms without opening doors into the halls. Large standpipes connected with these ladders run to the roof, with valves at every floor, and the whole house can be flooded with water, inside and outside, in one minute's time. The facilities, both for extinguishing fire and escaping from fire are equalled by no other house in the world.

No other House in the United States has better Water.

Every part of the House is neat, clean, and healthy.

Telegraph, Telephone, and Street Car connections.

STOP AT THE HARPER HOUSE WHEN YOU VISIT ROCK ISLAND.

Consort Life Company,

104 East Third Street,   **DAVENPORT, IOWA.**

Pays a death benefit from proceeds of an assessment on its membership, which membership can be taken in one or more of its four divisions (A, B, C, and D)—maximum benefit in each being limited to $2,000. . . . For husband and wife, in perfect health, the Joint Life Divisions, A or A and B, are first recommended, inasmuch as the Company takes the entire risk, and neither person insured need take thought which will die first, as the entire insurance paid for matures and becomes payable on the death of the *first* of the two lives insured. This plan not only affords the desired protection to the children, but also secures to the surviving parent, in old age, a competency which ought to be appreciated.

J. S. KEATOR, Pres.   S. J. KEATOR, Vice-Pres.   B. C. KEATOR, Sec. and Treas.

ESTABLISHED 1856.   INCORPORATED APRIL 15, 1881.

J. S. Keator Lumber Company

MANUFACTURERS OF AND DEALERS IN

GANG-SAWED LUMBER, LATH, AND SHINGLES.

Dimension Timber of any size sawed to order.   Estimates furnished on application.

Office, Cor. Water and Atkinson Sts.   **MOLINE, ILLINOIS.**

SMITH & STEARNS PAINT CO.

MAKERS OF

DRY COLORS,

S. & S. P. CO.

BRIGHT VERMILLION,

CHEMICALLY PURE.

CHROME YELLOWS,

PRIMERS AND PASTE PAINTS.

All the above specially adapted for use of Manufacturers of Agricultural Implements.

ALSO MANUFACTURERS OF

READY-MIXED PAINTS,

Guaranteed to be perfectly pure.   Write for Circulars.

SMITH & STEARNS PAINT CO.   **DAVENPORT, IOWA.**

INDEX OF CONTENTS.

A.

	PAGE.
Academy of Sciences,	62
Academy of the Immaculate Conception,	58
Ackley House,	61
Advantages, Manufacturing,	42
Appropriations by Congress,	23
Armstrong, Fort,	22
Arsenal, Rock Island, capacity of,	30
Association, Rock Island Business Men's,	66
Association, Y. M. C.,	64
Associations, Loan, Building, and Savings,	67
Asylum, Catholic Orphans',	64
Atmospheric Pressure,	70

B.

Banks, names and business of,	52
Barometer, means of,	73, 74
Bells, chime of,	65
Birds, the Island as a conservatory,	30, 31
Black Hawk,	18, 22. 68, 69
Black Hawk's Watch-Tower,	51, 67
Board of Trade, Davenport,	66
Board of Trade, Moline,	67
Bosse, Henry,	17
Bridges,	27
Burlington, distance to,	19
Burtis Opera House,	61

C.

Canal, Hennepin,	48
Cemetery, National,	35
Chicago, distance to,	19
Churches,	65
Climate,	72
Clock, Arsenal,	23
Cloudiness,	72
Coal Mines,	45
College, Augustana,	57
College, Davenport Business,	58
College, Griswold,	57
Congress, acts of,	23
Contents, table of,	11
Cook, Mrs. Clarissa C.,	60, 63
Cotton Goods, manufacture of,	43
Council Bluffs, distance to,	19

D.

Davenport City,	35
Davenport, Col. George,	23, 32
Davenport, Hon. Bailey,	68
Des Moines, distance to,	19
Drives, pleasure,	50
Dubuque, distance to,	19

E.

Educational Advantages,	57
Exchange, Davenp't Produce,	67

F.

Factories enumerated.	53
Ferry Boat,	51
Flagler, Col. D. W.,	17, 25, 30, 32
Frosts, table of earliest and latest,	76

G.

German Theater,	62

H.

Harper House,	61
Harper's Theater,	62
Hennepin Canal,	48
Home for the Friendless,	63
Home, Soldiers' Orphans',	62
Hospital, Mercy,	64
Hotels,	61
Humidity, relative, etc.,	71, 77

I.

Illustrations, list of,	12
Iron Mines,	45

K.

Kansas City, distance to,	19

Index of Contents.

Keator House, Moline, . 61
Kimball House, Davenport, 61
Kingsbury, Maj., ... 24

L.

Latitude and Longitude, . 19
Le Claire, Antoine, . . . 68
Legends, Indian, . . . 33, 34
Libraries, ... 60
Location of the Three Cities, 19
Lumber, amount floated by, 45

M.

Manufacturing Advantages, 38
Manufacturing Statistics, . 55
Martin, Capt. R. R., . 17, 70
Meteorology, ... 70
Middlemen discussed, . 42, 43
Mills enumerated, . . . 53
Milwaukee, distance to, . 19
Mississippi River, flow of water, 41
Moline City, ... 37
Moline Water Power Co., 37, 67

N.

Newcomb House, . . . 61
Newcomb, Mrs. P. V., . . 62
Newspapers, ... 56

O.

Opera Houses, . . . 61, 62
Orders, civic and benevolent, 66

P.

Peal's Hotel, ... 61
Peoria, distance to, . . . 19
Perry, Bishop, . . . 57, 65
Population, ... 19
Prison, Military, ... 34

R.

Railroads, ... 47
Rainfall, ... 71, 74, 75
Rock Island, . . . 20, 21
Rock Island City, ... 36
Rodman, Gen. T. J., . 23, 24
River, stage of, ... 76

S.

Schools, Davenport, . . . 58
Schools, Moline, ... 59
Schools, Rock Island, . . 59
Sciences, Academy of, . . 62
Seminary, Augustana Theo., 57
Seminary, St. Ambrose, . 58
Shoemaker, Capt., . . . 23
Shops, Armory and Arsenal, 26
Snowfalls, dates of, . . . 76
Societies, ... 65
Statistics, Manufacturing, . 55
Steamboats, ... 47
Street-Car Lines, ... 51
Street, Gen., ... 22
St. James Hotel, ... 61
St. Louis, distance to, . . 19
St. Paul, distance to, . . 19

T.

Telephone, system of, . . 51
Temperature, changes of, 72, 73
Trade, the wholesale, . . 55
Transportation Facilities, . 45

W.

Wagner's Opera House, . 62
Water Power, data of, . . 40
Wheelock, S. W., . . . 60
Wholesale Jobbing Houses, 55
Winds, prevalent, . . . 72
Woods, hard and soft, . . 45

INDEX OF ADVERTISEMENTS.

Architect— F. G. Clausen, 78
Attorneys— Ellis, Murphy & Gould, ... 85
Parks & Pleasants, . 78

Banks— Citizens National, Davenport, . . Cover
Davenport National, Cover
Davenport Savings, . 1

Banks—First Nat., Davpt., 14
  First National, Moline, Cover
  German Savings, . . 1
  Mitchell & Lynde, . . 90
  Moline National. .Cover
  Moline Savings. . Cover
  People's National, . . 90
  Rock Island National, 90
Boiler-Makers—Grupe & Murray, ... 3
Books, etc.,—Crampton & Co., 5
  Thompson & Carmichael, 84
Boots and Shoes (wholesale)—
  Bryant & Doe, . . 80
  (Retail)—G. M. Schmidt, 7
Box Factory—H. F. Moeller, 88
Candies, etc. (wholesale)—
  Reimers & Fernald, 89
  (Retail)—B. F. Taylor, 7
Carriages—J. L. Mason, . 81
Cattle—Thoroughbred Jerseys, 81
China and Crockery (wholesale)—J. Lorenzen, 80
Cigars and Tobacco—Otto Albrecht & Co., . . 82
  N. Kuhnen, ... 89
Cloths and Clothing (wholesale)—R. Krause, . 6
  (Retail)—I. Rothschild, 9
Coal and Lime—J. S. Wylie, 3
Commission House—M. D. Huggins, ... 82
Corn Planters—Deere & Mansur Co., ... 96
Crackers and Biscuit—J. M. Christy, ... 83
  Reupke, Schmidt & Co., 8
Dentists—Morgan & McCandless, ... 78
Drugs and Meds. (wholesale)
  —Hartz & Bahnsen, 90
Dry Goods (wholesale)—J. H. C. Petersen & Sons, 79
  W. C. Wadsworth & Co., 2
Elevators—Moline Elev. Co., 5

Flouring Mills—Phœnix Mills, 79
Foundry—Le Claire, . . 89
Furniture—C. C. Knell, . 78
  Smith & McCullough, . 7
  West Davenport Furniture Co., ... 83
Glucose Manufacturing Co., 7
Groceries (wholesale)—Beiderbecke & Miller, . 84
  Henry Dart's Sons, . 88
  (Retail)—Wm. Thompson, 8
Hardware (wholesale)—Sickels, Preston & Co., Cover
  Stewart & Montgomery, 91
  (Retail)—E. W. Spencer, 83
Hats and Caps—Cameron & Son, ... 78
Heating Co., Davenp't Steam, 6
Hotel—Harper House, . 91
Insurance—Consort Life, . 92
  E. W. Hurst, . . . 86
  Mississippi Valley Mutual, 96
Iron, Hardware (wholesale)—Sieg & Williams, . 81
Ladders—Davenport Ladder Co., ... 86
Livery Stables—Benton's. . 9
  M. M. Briggs, . . . 82
Lumber—Cable Lumber Co., 9
  Keator Lumber Co., . 92
Machinists—Ebi & Neuman, 79
  Williams, White & Co., 6
Malleable Iron—Union Malleable Iron Co., . . 10
Manufacturing Co., Barnard & Leas, ... 79
Music House—W. W. Kimball & Co., . . . 8
Oat Meal Co., Davenport, 78
Paints—Smith & Stearns, . 92
Photographs—Hastings, White & Fisher, ... 2
Plows—Deere & Co., . Cover
Pumps—Moline Pump Co., 85

Railroads — Chicago, Burling-
   ton & Quincy, . . 87
   Chicago, Rock Island &
      Pacific, ... 13
   Rock Island & Peoria, 87
Real Estate Agt.—C. H. Kent, 4
Sash, Doors, and Blinds—U.
   N. Roberts & Co., . 14
Saws — D. Donaldson, . . 84
Scales — Moline Scale Co., 89
Shirt Factory — G. R. Marvin, 6

Soaps — Warnock & Ralston, 84
Steamboat Lines—Diamond Jo, 85
   St. L. & St. P. Packet Co., 86
Stoves — E. W. Spencer, . 83
   Moline Stove Co., . . 82
Tailors — I. Rothschild, . 9
   Thos. McCullough & Son, 91
Toys, etc.—Berwald & Frisius, 9
Wagons—G. H. Young & Co., 88
   Moline Wagon Co., . 10
Woolen Mills, Davenport, . 80

DEERE & MANSUR CO.

MOLINE, ILLINOIS.

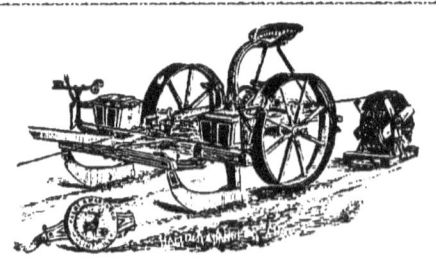

LARGEST PRODUCERS OF GOODS IN THEIR LINE IN THE COUNTRY.

LARGEST PRODUCERS OF GOODS IN THEIR LINE IN THE COUNTRY.

MANUFACTURERS OF THE CELEBRATED

Deere Rotary Drop Corn-Planter,

Deere Wire Check-Rower,

Deere and Moline Stalk-Cutters.

SEND FOR CIRCULARS.

Mississippi Valley Manufacturers Mutual Insurance Co.

ROCK ISLAND, ILLINOIS.

E. D. RAND, President.   WM. B. FERGUSON, Secretary.   J. M. GOULD, Treasurer.
WM. E. SMITH, Manager.

DIRECTORS.—J. S. KEATOR, J. S. Keator Lumber Co., Moline, Ill.; J. M. GOULD, President First National Bank, Moline, Ill.; S. H. VELIE, Deere & Co., Plow Works, Moline, Ill.; H. A. AINSWORTH, Williams, White & Co., Iron Works, Moline, Ill.; E. H. ANAWALT, Rock Island Lumber and Mfg. Co., Rock Island, Ill.; BENJ. HERSHEY, Hershey Lumber Co., Muscatine, Iowa; E. D. RAND, Burlington, Iowa; SILAS W. GARDINER, Gardiner, Batchelder & Willes, Lyons, Iowa; A. LAMB, Lamb & Sons, Clinton, Iowa; M. DONAHUE, Iron Works, Davenport, Iowa; C. M. SMITH, Bradner Smith & Co., Chicago; WM. P. BROWN, President Minnesota Millers Association, Red Wing, Minn.; C. B. SHOVE, Underwriter, Minneapolis, Minn.; WM. B. FERGUSON, Underwriter, Rock Island, Ill.; WM. E. SMITH, Underwriter, Rock Island, Ill.

ROBERT SICKELS.　　　　J. R. PRESTON.　　　　J. R. NUTTING.

SICKELS, PRESTON & CO.
HARDWARE.

226 West Second Street — Retail.

121 and 123 West Third Street — Wholesale.

DAVENPORT, IOWA.

J. M. GOULD, Pres.　　CHAS. ATKINSON, Vice-Pres.　　JOHN S. GILLMORE, Cashier.

FIRST NATIONAL BANK,
MOLINE, ILLINOIS.

Organized, December, 1863.　　Charter extended, February 24, 1883.

Capital, - **$100,000.** | **Surplus,** - **$30,000.**

Collections given prompt and careful attention, and remitted for at lowest rates on day of payment.

DIRECTORS.—J. M. Gould, Chas. Atkinson, John Deere, Jas. Shaw, Jonathan Huntoon, D. C. Dimock, J. T. Browning, Chas. H. Deere, Samuel Bowles, H. A. Barnard, Porter Skinner, Morris Rosenfield, John S. Gillmore.

CORRESPONDENTS.—Northwestern National Bank, Chicago; Importers and Traders National Bank, New York.

MOLINE NATIONAL BANK,
MOLINE, ILLINOIS.

Capital, - **$100,000.** | **Surplus,** - **$20,000.**

S. W. WHEELOCK, President.　　PORTER SKINNER, Vice-President.
C. F. HEMENWAY, Cashier.

Directors.—S. W. Wheelock, Porter Skinner, H. A. Barnard, J. Silas Leas, Hiram Darling, N. Chester, A. S. Wright, Ezra Smith, J. M. Christy, L. E. Hemenway, C. Vitzthum, J. S. Keator, C. F. Hemenway.

DOES A GENERAL BANKING BUSINESS.

MOLINE SAVINGS BANK,
MOLINE, ILLINOIS.

Chartered by the State Legislature. The Only Chartered Savings Bank in Rock Island County.

S. W. WHEELOCK, President.　　　　PORTER SKINNER, Vice-President.
C. F. HEMENWAY, Cashier.

Trustees.—S. W. Wheelock, Porter Skinner, H. A. Barnard, J. Silas Leas, Hiram Darling, N. Chester, A. S. Wright, Ezra Smith, J. M. Christy, L. E. Hemenway, C. Vitzthum, C. F. Hemenway.

INTEREST ALLOWED AT FOUR PER CENT.

www.ingramcontent.com/pod-product-compliance
Lightning Source LLC
Chambersburg PA
CBHW030410170426
43202CB00010B/1556